DIVINE ORDER

IN THE CHURCH

A Study of First Corinthians

Pathway

PRESS & RESOURCES

DIVINE ORDER
IN THE CHURCH

A Study of First Corinthians

FRENCH L. ARRINGTON

Managing Editor of Publications: Lance Colkmire
Editorial Assistant: Tammy Hatfield
Graphic Design and Layout: Michael McDonald

ISBN: 978-1-64288-035-9

Copyright © 2018 by Pathway Press
Revision of the 1998 edition
1080 Montgomery Avenue
Cleveland, Tennessee 37311

Visit *www.pathwaypress.org* for more information.
Printed in the United States of America

DEDICATION

To Mother and my students, past and present.

CONTENTS

CHAPTER 1

THE CITY AND THE CHURCH

Grave troubles were in the church at Corinth. Paul, the founder of that church, was called upon to deal with an extraordinary array of difficulties among the Corinthian converts. After his initial stay there, he carried on an extended correspondence with them in which he offered instructions that would hopefully set the affairs of the church in order.

One of his epistles to them is now known as First Corinthians. Fittingly, the emphasis of that entire epistle is practical Christian living. The converts from paganism found it exceedingly difficult to understand the high moral standards of the Gospel and to overcome the besetting temptation of their former lifestyle. By grappling with the deteriorating circumstances in which they were enmeshed, Paul provided an unparalleled view of the everyday life in an early first-century church and of his endeavor to give spiritual direction to an unruly congregation.

If we appreciate the relevance of 1 Corinthians for our day, we must first understand its meaning for Paul's day. One way to gain a proper perspective is to examine the atmosphere that persisted in Corinth in the middle of the first century and to determine the nature of the urgent problems facing the Corinthian believers. Hopefully, the following discussion will give us a picture of the conditions at Corinth.

The City of Corinth

Corinth has been called "the Vanity Fair in the ancient world." To say the least, licentious excesses were commonplace. The character of the city and its inhabitants were reflected in the Corinthian believers and helped create the troubles in the local Christian community. Paul had preached to them the word of the Cross (1 Cor. 15:1-4), which is able to transform life. The ultimate success of Christianity in Corinth is a tribute to the power of the Gospel. A number of factors made that pagan city what it was when Paul first arrived there.

Its History. Corinth had existed for more than a thousand years before Paul's time, and was one of the famous and important cities of the ancient world. In 146 BC the city was reduced to ashes by the Roman general Lucius Mummius. The residents were either killed or sold into slavery. Because rebuilding was forbidden, the city lay in ruins for a century; but Julius Caesar recognized its strategic military value. At his command, the city was rebuilt in 46-44 BC. At first the citizens of the new city were Roman freedmen, but the population quickly became cosmopolitan and included a community of Jews. So there the East met the West and freely exchanged their ideas and ideals and material goods. By the time of Paul, the city had become the capital of the Roman province of Achaia which, along with the province of Macedonia, encompassed the whole of Greece.

The new Corinth was three and one-half miles northeast of the old city. By the time Paul arrived (AD 50-52), the population of the city had grown to 500,000. Other than its location in the same general area, the new city at first had little similarity to the old. No sooner had the city been rebuilt than it began to develop its individuality and regain much of its earlier greatness. In 1859 the ruins of the old city were destroyed by an earthquake. If we were to visit the site of ancient Corinth today, we would see a few columns of the temple of Apollo, the Greek god of poetry and prophecy.

These columns stand as a mute testimony to the city before it was leveled to the ground by Mummius.

Its Geography. Few cities were located in a more impressive setting. A look at the map will show that Corinth was a city of Greece and stood on a four-mile-wide strip of land, called an *isthmus* (from the Greek, especially for "a neck of land between two seas"). If there had been no isthmus, the southern part of Greece would have been an island.

As well as forming a long bridge between the north and south, the isthmus was an important link for ocean-going vessels between east and west. Until the completion of the Corinth Canal in 1893[1] merchants and sailors preferred to haul their cargoes across the isthmus rather than endure the long trip and risk the dangerous waters around the southern tip of Greece.[2] Small ships and cargo from large ships were transported safely over the small strip of land by a form of trolley car on crude wooden rails.

Corinth was a crossroads. All the traffic from the north and from the south in Greece had to pass through the city. Through it also flowed much of the traffic between the east and west. So the Corinth that Paul marched into was in one of the greatest trading and commerce centers in the Roman Empire. Competition in business was keen. The minds of the people dwelt on moneymaking, and the order of the day was buying and selling in the marketplace.

Furthermore, the city of Corinth was situated in quite a metropolitan area. Athens was less than fifty miles away. Around Corinth clustered three towns: just one and one-half miles to the north lay

---

[1] In A.D. 67 Nero with forced labor, including Jewish captives attempted to cut a canal through the isthmus but without success.

[2] The treachery and distance of a voyage around the Greek peninsula were well known, as indicated by the proverb: "Let him who sails around Malea first make his will" (quoted by William Barclay in *The Letters to the Corinthians*).

Lechaeum; seven and one-half miles to the east, Cenchrea; just a short distance away, Schoenus. Both Lechaeum and Cenchrea had a harbor, giving Corinth a seaport on each side.

The city was a sailor's paradise. Much like some of the urban centers in modern America, Corinth was known for its flourishing wealth and pleasure. What New York and San Francisco are to the United States, what Paris is to France, and what Hong Kong is to the Orient, Corinth was to Macedonia and Asia Minor. It was a boomtown, a crossroads of travel and commerce. There competition in business was fierce. Sparing no means, men and women fought to gain the spoils of prosperity. Reckless individualism was the Corinthian ideal. Nothing was barred. They recognized no law but their own desires.

The city needed the purifying influence of the Gospel. No doubt, Paul was aware of its lurid reputation, but that was not the overriding factor that brought him to Corinth. Its geographical location was what induced Paul to preach the Gospel there. Much of the population of the city was mobile. Merchants and travelers came and went. The situation of Corinth made it the ideal place to establish a church. From that important center could radiate the Gospel unto the surrounding regions. So it was certain that Paul's preaching would have wide circulation.

Its Notoriety. Corinth was a city of wealth and pleasure. The ancient city destroyed by the Romans in 146 BC had become the butt of jokes. The debauchery of Corinth was proverbial; the term *Corinthianize* was coined to refer to licentious excesses. The morals of the people were deplorably low; the name of the city became a synonym for immorality, debauchery, and vice. It was said that those who led loose and scandalous lives played the Corinthian.

Unfortunately, by Paul's time Corinth had regained its fame for wickedness, and the same atmosphere that had prevailed in the ancient city prevailed in Paul's day. Prominent among the problems that Paul had to deal with was laxity in sexual matters. So the morals of the new city were no better than the old.

To use modern parlance, Corinth was a haven for playboys and prostitutes. On the highest point in the city stood the pagan temple of Aphrodite, the Greek goddess of beauty and love. Attached to that temple were a thousand women prostitutes serving as priestesses. At evening time these women went into Corinth to ply their trade and to entertain in the night life of the city. The people of Corinth, therefore, were notoriously profligate. They laughed at wickedness rather than restraining it, and turned freedom into license. No doubt, some of the residents were repulsed by the evils and the lust in the city, but apparently they lacked the influence and stamina to resist the plague of immorality, vice, debauchery, and filth.

Corinthian society was thoroughly pagan. Every man chose his own philosophy of life, and his religion permitted him to do whatever he desired with a clear conscience. No one took his philosophy too seriously. Free thinking and intellectual superficiality were common. Shallow thought was apparent in childish conceit and love for skillful words and philosophical jargon.

Wealth was the supreme god. The reckless wastefulness of those who had money made the place so expensive that it became a saying, "It is not for everyone to go to Corinth." With wealth they could have done much good—promoted art and literature and improved life in general or helped the less fortunate, many of whom barely existed, living in the wretchedness of extreme poverty. All of these uses for money would have been noble, but none of them were the overriding motive behind the Corinthians' unrestrained enthusiasm for moneymaking. Wealth was the means to pleasure—to wine, women, and song. For the most part, the Corinthians were occupied with "making money and making love."[3] Thus, in an atmosphere laden with moral corruption, it is

---

[3] Cited by Russell P. Spittler, *The Corinthian Correspondence*, p. 11.

little wonder that the early believers in Corinth were, to some extent, affected by the prevailing influence.

PAUL'S MINISTRY IN CORINTH

The church was founded by Paul, probably about AD 50. On his second missionary journey, he arrived in Corinth from Athens (Acts 18:1-18). He became fast friends with a godly couple, Aquila and Priscilla, who were among the Jews recently expelled from Rome by an anti-Semitic decree of Emperor Claudius. Like Paul, they were tentmakers. While in Corinth, Paul supported himself by working with Aquila and Priscilla at their common craft (1 Cor. 9:14, 15; 2 Cor. 12:13). Too, he took lodging with them, and they became his coworkers in the Gospel.

Paul remained in town for about two years. As his custom was, he sought out the synagogue. There, from Sabbath to Sabbath, he preached Jesus as the Christ. When Silas and Timothy arrived from Macedonia to help him, he gave himself exclusively to preaching the Gospel. His labors were richly rewarded. Both Jews and Gentile proselytes were convinced and believed. This included even Crispus, the ruler of the synagogue, along with his family (Acts 18:4, 8). Can we imagine two groups, Jews and Christians, going to the same place at the same time to worship? Indeed, there were problems. Paul himself was forced by the Jews from the synagogue. He left with the declaration: "Your blood be upon your own heads; I am clean: from henchforth I will go unto the Gentiles" (Acts 18:6).

The apostle moved his ministry into the home of Justus, which was near the Jewish synagogue. When Crispus, the ruler of the synagogue, and others deserted the Jewish synagogue to join the Christian fellowship next door, feelings against the Christians must have become intense. An encouraging vision was granted to Paul in which God assured him that many would be converted through his ministry.

The Corinthian mission continued. Finally the Jews' bitterness toward Paul expressed itself in a threat on his life. They brought him before the Roman proconsul, Gallio, and complained that he was advising people to worship God contrary to the law of Moses. Knowing Roman law, the proconsul recognized that the charges were not concerned with a misdemeanor or a serious crime and that Paul was no lawbreaker. The dispute was one of questions of their own law. So Gallio showed no concern whatsoever and refused to hear the case.

After that the apostle stayed on in Corinth for some time. But the Holy Spirit moved him to turn his eyes on the province of Asia. With Aquila and Priscilla, he departed from Corinth and stopped briefly at Ephesus, a metropolis of Asia, where he left his two friends. Then he set sail for Antioch in Syria.

One other visit is recorded in the Book of Acts (20:1-3). On his third missionary journey, Paul revisited the city of Corinth. No details of that visit are given, but it was just prior to his final visit to Jerusalem. Some are convinced that Paul's second visit was his last time in Corinth. However, in 2 Corinthians 13:1, he spoke as if his last visit was a third visit. It is not completely clear that he came to Corinth for a third visit. He did postpone a visit so that he might not be present to blame them more severely (2 Cor. 1:23).

THE CHURCH AT CORINTH

The Corinthian Church was a problem congregation. There was discrepancy between the Lord and His church. Many among the Corinthian believers had gone astray from Christian living, proper order in worship, and sound doctrine. Paul, their father in the Lord, recognized that the moral health and spiritual life of the church were threatened. Our understanding of the dangers should be enhanced by noting the social classes and groups in the Corinthian congregation and the errors that developed among them.

Its Different Groups. The Corinthian Church was comprised of many different groups, each of which followed the natural tendency to blend old habits and beliefs with their Christian experience. From Paul's writing, we discern that there were both Jews and Gentiles in the church, the latter perhaps being predominant.

No doubt, among the members of the community were freedmen and slaves (1 Cor. 7:21). It is clear that the members came largely from the lower classes (1 Cor. 1:26; 6:11; 7:21). There were not many among them wise by human standards, not many influential and powerful, and not many nobly born (1 Cor. 1:26). God had delighted in making "somebodies" out of "nobodies."

However, a few of the Christians there were prominent people. Among them were Crispus, the ruler of the synagogue, and Erastus and Gaius, men of prominence and means (Acts 18:8; Rom. 16:23). Therefore, the congregation included Jews and Gentiles, bond and free, rich and poor, and educated and ignorant. That was as it should have been. The Gospel is for all people, regardless of their station in life.

Its Troubles. For Paul the Christian fellowship at Corinth was a source of joy and trial. He addressed the fellowship as "the church of God . . . sanctified in Christ . . . called to be saints" (1 Cor. 1:2). But the believers' religious and philosophical differences created problems for the young church; such as factions among them, the belief that the kingdom of God had fully come and that they were already living in the end-time,[4] abuse of Christian freedom, and vying with one another in exercising spiritual gifts. All of these troubled Paul.

Since the habits of paganism clung to many, there was no clear-cut break with the world. "The Church was in the world, as it had

---

[4] Note especially 1 Corinthians 4:8. Furthermore, for an exposition that understands that all the problems dealt with in 1 Corinthians are symptoms of the problem of over-realized eschatology, see French L. Arrington, *Paul's Aeom Theology in 1 Corinthians.*

to be, but the world was in the Church, as it ought not to be."[5] So the influence of the pagan city and diverse elements in the church tended to rip it apart.

Cliques or parties had been formed with the church. The snobbish factions rallied around the names of Paul, Apollos, Peter, or even of Christ, and pledged their loyalty to one or the other.

Too, there was a case of the worst kind of fornication among them. Viewing it as harmless, the church had taken no steps to discipline the offender.

There were also some Christians that took one another into courts, and others were guilty of sexual impurity.

Such gross sins had crept into the church. To make matters worse, there were irregularities in worship and sound doctrine, particularly the resurrection of the dead. Paul was called upon to deal with grave evils and to offer spiritual guidance directed to the immediate needs of the Corinthian Church. Paul dealt with these problems, which have a way of recurring in every age and every place. But, more importantly, he offered the basis for meaningful and holy living.

This is seen in a number of specifics. First, he offered Christ, the sum and substance of the Gospel. Second, he offered a way of life that makes us responsible for what we do and the influence we have on others. Third, he offered the power of the crucified, risen Christ to enable us to live in harmony with one another. Fourth, he offered a spirit of tolerance and mutual upbuilding, grounded in redemptive love. Fifth, he offered a program of stewardship and unselfish service.

These great truths will be amplified as we study Paul's challenge to the Corinthians to bring their lives into conformity with their

---

[5] James Moffatt, *Commentary on 1 Corinthians* (*The Moffatt New Testament Commentary*), p. xv.

high position in Christ. What a challenge the truths of the Gospel were to the Christians in the pagan city of Corinth! What a challenge they are to us in our pagan world!

THE OCCASION AND PURPOSE

This epistle was written on the apostle's third missionary journey. At the climax of his second missionary journey, he established the church at Corinth. Then he returned to his home church in Antioch of Syria by way of Ephesus. "After he had spent some time there, he departed, and went over all the country of Galatia and Phrygia . . . strengthening all the disciples" (Acts 18:23). This began his third missionary journey.

During Paul's absence from Ephesus, Apollos, an Alexandrian Jew, visited that city and met Aquila and Priscilla. After they expounded to him more accurately the way of God, he traveled to Corinth were he probably served as pastor for several months (Acts 18:24-28).

While Apollos was in Corinth, Paul arrived in Ephesus, where he ministered for the next three years. Many believe that shortly after Paul reached Ephesus, he sent a short letter, now lost, to the church at Corinth (1 Cor. 5:9). Scholars refer to it as "the previous letter." We are not certain of the problems dealt with in the missing letter, but the gist of them is reflected in the admonition "not to . . . [associate] with fornicators." The troubles at Corinth became more aggravated. Because of this, Apollos left the city and joined Paul in Ephesus.

The situation at Corinth continued to degenerate. Soon members of the household of Chloe arrived in Ephesus from Corinth with a firsthand report about the troubled state of their home church (1 Cor. 1:11). Boasts were made that wisdom was imparted to the spirituals, not to ordinary men. Such pretentious claims created fiery antagonisms. The church was on the verge of shattering, with each faction zealously devoted to a different leader—Paul,

Peter, Apollos, or Christ. Each faction thought of itself as the spiritual elite. This led them to disdain others and to jeopardize the existence of the church (1 Cor. 1:10—4:21).

Moreover, one member of the congregation was living with his stepmother without objection from the church (1 Cor. 5:1-13). Some Christians were suing one another in pagan court (1 Cor. 6:1-8). Others were patronizing houses of ill-fame (1 Cor. 6:9-20).

The first six chapters of 1 Corinthians dealt with the oral report by Chloe's people. In the remaining chapters, Paul shifted his attention to a letter from the Corinthians. Someone had the idea of bringing Paul back into the picture and sent him a letter. Perhaps the letter was brought by the hands of Stephanas, Fortunatus, and Achaicus, who were members of the congregation at Corinth (1 Cor. 16:17). In it, various questions were asked about such moral and doctrinal matters as marriage, contact with the world, worship, and the Resurrection. Therefore, by conversations with Apollos, Chloe's people, and the three church members (plus the content of the letter), Paul learned about the troubles in the church.

At that time Paul was unable to leave Ephesus. He pleaded with Apollos to return to Corinth, but to no avail (1 Cor. 16:12). Sensing the problems were urgent enough to require an immediate answer, he wrote 1 Corinthians. The Epistle was probably composed near the end of Paul's stay at Ephesus (Acts 19:1, 21), because he had already made plans to visit Corinth (1 Cor. 16:5). It is impossible to determine the exact year of composition, but it was "not earlier than 55 and not later than 57."[6]

The purpose of this significant epistle is clear. In the interest of unity, Paul rebuked the dissensions, disorders, and errors among the believers and answered a letter of inquiry from Corinth. He

---

[6] *Ibid.*

dealt with their problems with the reminder that "God is not the author of confusion, but of peace, as in all churches of the saints" (1 Cor. 14:33). He gave explicit instructions as to how they may ensure that "all things be done decently and in order" (1 Cor. 14:40). To put it another way, 1 Corinthians offers the prescription for divine order in the church.

The problems that this inspired epistle addresses were problems in the first-century church, particularly at Corinth; but, in one form or another, they still more or less are common to the church today. It is as urgent now as it was then that in the church all things be done in a becoming and orderly manner.

CHAPTER 2

AN APPEAL FOR HARMONY
(1:1—4:1)

Before treating the many problems that beset the Corinthian Church, the apostle reminded the believers of their position in Christ. Their fellowship in the church was centered in Him. However, theirs was more than a local fellowship; it was part of that universal fellowship of which Christ is Lord. Indeed, He is Lord of one and all who willingly recognize His Lordship through their fellowship with Him and obedience to His will.

But the Corinthians had failed to consecrate themselves to Christ as Lord. They had been set apart (sanctified) and empowered to be God's holy people (1:2), but their heavenly standing and consecration in Christ had not made them Christlike. From every indication, practical holiness could not be discerned among them. Errors and imperfections prevailed in the church. The intent of the enemy was to destroy from without and from within that fellowship of believers.

Before turning the searchlight on the church, Paul offered thanks to God that they had been endowed with all spiritual gifts (vv. 4-7). The abundance of their spiritual blessing called forth his thanksgiving. Before correction he gave commendation. That is admirable in any minister. Commendation of people and their strengths serves to create a positive response to correction.

DISSENSIONS AMONG THE FAITHFUL

The apostle began to deal with one of many problems at Corinth: factions had created a serious breach in the church's fellowship. Believers had fallen victim to the plague of disunity. Paul introduced the subject with a tender appeal rather than with an apostolic demand. "Now I beseech you, brethren, by the name of our Lord Jesus Christ, that ye all speak the same thing, and that there be no divisions among you; but that ye be perfectly joined together in the same mind and in the same judgment" (1:10).

He addressed the Corinthians as "brethren." By the use of that word, Paul did two things: First, he softened the rebuke. His rebuke was not that of a schoolmaster with a rod, but that of one who had no feeling other than brotherly love. Second, he showed how wrong the divisions among them were. They were brethren and members of the same family. What should have persisted in their fellowship was love that abounded toward one another. But there were schisms—brothers set against brothers in the church.

A *Party Spirit* (vv. 10-13). On the basis of their spiritual understanding, Paul urged them to strive for unity. Their differences led to quarrels and bitterness because each held that his opinion was the only right one and each discredited the views of the others. "Speak[ing] the same thing" does not suggest that minor differences of opinion may not exist. But Paul admonished them to agree on the essentials to give a united testimony to the unbelieving world. So that they might present a solid front, Paul exhorted them to be perfectly joined together in the same mind and in the same judgment. The occasion for such an exhortation to unity was a report from Chloe's household that brought to Paul's attention divisions within the church. There were rival groups; each had its party slogans: "I am of Paul . . . I [am] of Apollos . . . I [am] of Cephas (Peter) . . . I [am] of Christ" (v. 12). The church was rent with "divisions" (*schismata*, "schisms" or "cliques"), which centered on their ministers.

There were those who professed to follow Paul. He was their spiritual father, and they were "charter members" of the church at Corinth. Like Paul, they emphasized justification by faith and freedom from the Law.

Others claimed to belong to Apollos, the learned and eloquent Bible student from Alexandria. They had never heard a pulpit man like Apollos.

Some of the believers, however, were loyal to Peter. There is no record of Peter's missionary effort in Corinth. Perhaps some of his converts in Judea moved to Corinth. They were conservative Jewish believers who considered the preacher at Pentecost to be a more authoritative apostle than Paul and advocated the superiority of the Jerusalem apostles.

Apparently there was also a faction that did not acknowledge either Paul, Apollos, or Peter. They claimed Christ himself as their teacher and leader. Did not all Christians belong to Christ? There should have been no doubt: "Ye are bought with a price" (6:20).

Why they laid exclusive claim is uncertain. They might have known and followed Him during His earthly ministry; therefore, they felt superior to Paul or the Christians who had not companied with Christ. Or they could have named themselves after Christ because they claimed to have fellowship with Him by visions and revelations. Out of motives of snobbery, the believers confessed to be of Paul, Apollos, Peter, or even of Christ. The truth was that they were of the flesh.

Paul was grieved that some took his name and gathered around it. So he asked, "Is Christ divided? Was Paul crucified for you? or were ye baptized in the name of Paul?" (1:13). The obvious answer to all of these was no. In light of the contentions and divisions among them, it could have been assumed the answer was yes. The point was that Christ was not divided into fragments and parceled out among the competing groups. There was only one undivided

Christ. If a man belonged to Him, it was trivial to attach himself to Paul, Apollos, or Peter.

The members of the church had no right to be divided into parties. Christ was not divided, but the Corinthian church was. None other than Christ died for them; it was in His name that they were baptized. There was but One whose name they should bear and to whom they should yield in submission—the One crucified for them and under whose authority they were baptized. They had utterly lost sight of the glory of the Lord and His saving work through the Cross.

Party Labels *(vv. 14-17).* Paul was not guilty of recruiting followers, for he had baptized no more than a few converts. If the words about baptism here are ripped out of context, it appears that Paul disparaged the ordinance of water baptism. But no doubt he left it to his coworkers to baptize the converts, as Jesus may have done (cf. John 4:1-3). God sent Paul to preach; preaching the message of the Cross was primary. He was glad that he had not baptized more of the Corinthians, thereby giving them cause to claim a Pauline party. Their loyalty to Paul would then have been exceeded by their loyalty to Christ.

Christ was the only cure for the problems among the Corinthians. His name is mentioned no fewer than ten times in the first ten verses of the first chapter. The church may be tempted to deal with difficult circumstances by law or human understanding and compassion; but the most effective approach is to deal with them as Paul did at Corinth—in light of the Cross and Christ's love. Among believers, unity is found in Jesus Christ and is essentially Christ-centered. Ministers must see to it that their ministry draws men to Christ.

THE TRUE WISDOM AND THE FALSE

Men exalt men. They exalt what they know or how well they can communicate what they know. But Paul the apostle examined such human wisdom in light of the Gospel.

The Power of God (1:18—2:5). That the Gospel is not worldly wisdom, but the power of God is shown in three ways: (1) by the experience of those Corinthians who had received it (1:18-25); (2) by the makeup of the church (vv. 26-31); and (3) by Paul's attitude and method when he came to them (2:1-5).

First, the knowledge and eloquence of the wise were not responsible for the Corinthians' salvation. That which was responsible was the message of Christ's crucifixion, which was sheer nonsense to those on their way to destruction; but for those being saved it was the power of God.

Christians know the Cross is the power and wisdom of God; even the Corinthian converts knew it. The world of the first century was divided into Jews and Greeks. The Jews asked for a sign; they were the miracle-hunters. For a Messiah to die in shame and impotence on a cross was outrageous to them.

Moreover, the Greeks (Gentiles, non-Jewish world) searched for wisdom. The Cross had no place in their learned and endless discussions. For them the preaching of the Cross was crude, and intellectually it made no sense. It was foolish and moronic, so they thought, because it required no high intellectual gift, but only simple faith in the crucified and risen Savior.

But to the saved Jews and Gentiles it was God's power and wisdom. Why? What God did in Christ accomplished what human wisdom and power had not—salvation from sin. What appeared as folly did disclose truth about God. What seemed to be weakness did deliver people from the power of sin and destroyed what nothing else could destroy. Indeed, for believers the gospel of the Cross becomes the highest wisdom and the greatest power. It is logical to people of faith because they have experienced its transforming power.

Second, when God called them into fellowship with Christ, few of the Christians at Corinth were of high social standing. By human standards not many were wise, influential, powerful, or noble. God chose the foolish, weak, and despised in the world so that He might put to shame the world's wise and strong men. He even purposely chose what did not exist to bring to nought what did exist. That is the truth! When Paul first came to Corinth, there had been no church in the city, but now it existed. The only explanation for that was God's creative grace, which made "somebodies" out of "nobodies."

More than the humiliation of the world's pride, God had a purpose within the body of Christ—"That no flesh should glory [boast] in his presence" (1:29). It was not the world's pride that prompted Paul to write to Corinth, but boasting within the church. They were glorying in men and had forgotten the Christian life rests on the grace of God. Paul reminded them that all their gifts and spiritual possessions (wisdom, righteousness, sanctification, and redemption) came from God. "[Therefore] as it is written . . . [if any wants to boast], let him . . . [boast about] the Lord" (v. 31).

Third, in evangelizing the Corinthians, Paul did not rely on skillful words of human wisdom.[1] This does not suggest that he did not employ proper speech and a kind of wisdom. But he kept the Cross in the foreground and his eloquence and wisdom in the background. Among the wisdom-loving Corinthians, he determined to preach nothing but Christ and His death on the cross.

His preaching was not impressive. He stood before the Corinthians at first in great "weakness . . . and . . . trembling" (2:3). He realized his own insufficiency. Thus, he came not with the bearing of a distinguished man, relying on his accomplishments and prestige for success, but with a sense of total dependence on the Holy Spirit.

Effective preaching does not exclude the use of human knowledge

---

[1] This may seem strange for him to say since the diction of Romans 8 and 1 Corinthians 13 are comparable to some of the best classical literature, but his intention was to help the Corinthians understand that human eloquence was not as important as they thought.

or individual talent, neither does it give place to showmanship. In fact, Paul's preaching was not directed by persuasive words of human wisdom; that is, it was not shaped and regulated by skillful words!

What he preached was regulated by the Cross and furthermore, accompanied by the Spirit and power. Through the preaching of the Gospel the powerful Holy Spirit gripped the Corinthians' hearts and brought them to repentance and faith. The faith of his hearers did not stand in the wisdom of men, but in the power of God (v. 4). In no way could Corinthian believers boast in Paul's ability. They had nothing to glory in except Christ alone. If they all glorified Christ their party loyalties would begin to fade away.

The True Wisdom of God (2:6—3:4). The apostle was not adverse to the right kind of wisdom. "Among them that are perfect [mature]," he declared, "we speak wisdom," although it is not mere human wisdom. It is "the [hidden] wisdom of God."

Such wisdom is revealed by God (2:6-9). It is intended for the spiritually mature Christian, who, as explained in verse 12, does not receive the spirit of the world, but the Spirit that comes from God. He is the spiritual man (v. 15).

All the Corinthian believers were not what they should have been. By their dissensions, the Corinthians disclosed that they were neither mature nor spiritual, but still infants. There was no simple gospel of the Cross for infants and a different, wisdom gospel for the mature. Paul described what he preached as "the wisdom of God in a mystery [secret]," which refers specifically to Christ crucified. "It signifies a secret," Morris says, "which man is wholly unable to penetrate. But it is a secret which God has now revealed."[2] God's wisdom was revealed in the cross-death, but for the unbeliever it remains hidden.

From the beginning God purposed to redeem humankind. The wisdom of God disclosed in the Cross leads to "our glory

---

[2] Morris, *op.cit.*, p. 55.

[our salvation]" (v. 7), but it brings the "princes of this world [literally, rulers of this age]" (v. 8) to nothing. The rulers of this age, it is assumed, were Pilate, Herod, and the Sanhedrin—collaborating in the death of Jesus; but demonic powers stood behind the political and religious authorities and conspired to bring Jesus to His death.

Through the Cross, Christ triumphed over powers and principalities (Col. 2:15) and defeated the ruler of this world (John 12:31). The wisdom revealed by God had never been discovered by mere human intellect. What God has prepared is unseen, unheard, and unthought by human wisdom.

Spiritual truth is taught by the Holy Spirit to hearts that are open to Him (1 Cor. 2:10-13). No one but the Holy Spirit reveals the truth of God. The truths of God are given through the preaching of the Word and in the inspired Scriptures. Only the human spirit can really know what is in the heart of a man. Likewise, only God can know and communicate truths about Himself.

God knows His purposes as the spirit of man knows his. He reveals them through His Spirit. Therefore, the Christian has received the indwelling presence of the Holy Spirit "that we might know the things that are freely given to us of God" (v. 12).

Paul's effectiveness among the Corinthians was due to the enlightening aid of the Spirit, enabling him to speak "not in the words which man's wisdom teacheth, but which the Holy Ghost teacheth" (v. 13). His utterances, as well as his thoughts, were Spirit-controlled.

By the Holy Spirit the spiritual man is taught the deep truths of God and empowered to proclaim them. This is accomplished by the Spirit through people. Thus God is to be praised; not men.

The Corinthians were not controlled by the Spirit; they boasted in men, not in God. Paul divided the human family into three categories: the natural man (v. 14), the spiritual man (vv. 15-16), and the carnal man (3:1-4). The natural man is unsaved and does not perceive spiritual truths because the indwelling presence and teaching ministry of the Holy Spirit are outside of his experience. The spiritual man is not only saved but is yielded to the indwelling Spirit. Thus, he welcomes all spiritual truth, the wisdom of God, which the Holy Spirit chooses to impart to him. The carnal man is also saved, but is not yielded to the Spirit. Because he thinks and acts like an unsaved man, he is in danger of slipping away from the Savior.

The divisions among Corinthians marked a carnal state of their hearts. They could not be spoken to as "spiritual," for they were "carnal" (v. 1). Not yet were they in the position to be instructed by the Spirit of God. "There is among you," wrote Paul, "envying, and strife, and divisions, are ye not carnal, and walk as men? For while one saith, I am of Paul; and another, I am of Apollos; are ye not carnal?" (vv. 3-4).

THE PLACE OF CHRISTIAN MINISTERS

The apostle desired to weld the party-torn church at Corinth into an army for the Lord. He attempted to improve the Corinthian situation by discussing the message Christians were to receive. Turning to the place of leaders in the church, he sought to correct the Corinthians' misunderstanding of the ministry.

The Ministry of Paul and Apollos (vv. 5-9). These men were instruments, by the grace of God, to win the Corinthians to faith. To Paul and Apollos, God had assigned a task; each had performed his duty. All the gifts and powers they had exercised in the work of the ministry were given them by God. The Corinthians regarded Paul and Apollos as competitors, vying with one another, as traveling teachers often did in that day.

To establish a real purpose of the ministry Paul used two pictures: one from agriculture, the other from construction. He said,

"I have planted, Apollos watered; but God gave the increase" (v. 6). Because Paul was the first evangelist to work in Corinth, he likened himself to one who plants. Apollos came later and continued the work of evangelism; he assumed the duties of tending and watering the crop.

Neither of these servants made the plants grow. God gave the increase—the success and growth. Through the preaching of the Gospel, Paul led souls to Jesus Christ, and Apollos built up those who believed in the Savior. The success and effectiveness of both were due not to their capabilities but to the blessing of God on their labor. Apart from God's blessings, they could not have been a blessing.

Therefore, neither he who plants nor he who waters is anything but a human instrument dependent on the blessing of God: "God gave the increase." No man can take credit for that. Although the man who plants and the man who waters have subordinate roles as far as church growth is concerned, both are one and equal in their labor. Paul and Apollos worked as partners, not as rivals. One was not superior to the other, as the Corinthians mistakenly assumed. Ministers are not to compete with each other but are to complement each other, for we belong to God as fellow workers with one another (v. 9).

The Responsibility of the Builders of the Church (vv. 10-15). Paul shifted the metaphor from agriculture to construction. He described the work of the ministry in architectural terms—foundation, building, and builder. As pioneer evangelist, Paul, like a master builder, had laid the ground work for the new church in Corinth. When Paul described himself as a "wise masterbuilder," he was careful to include the phrase "according to the grace of God" (v. 10).

The word *masterbuilder* literally rendered is an "architect." This position was not one of himself. The construction of the church was not due to his own skill in drawing up the blueprints and selecting the materials for the building. What he did was according to the grace that God had bestowed on him. God had called him by His grace, qualified him by His grace, and by His grace was pleased to use him to establish churches in unevangelized places.

There are two ways a builder can go wrong: by laying a poor foundation and by using inferior materials. Paul made it clear that the Church has only one true foundation—Jesus Christ himself. It is possible to build a community on another foundation, but such would not be a church.

Those who ministered after Paul built on the one foundation. However, some used inferior building materials—wood, hay, and stubble: these represented the teachings that they added to Paul's proclamation of Christ crucified.

The Day of Judgment will reveal each minister's contribution to the life of the Church. If he has included only sound building materials—gold, silver, and precious stones (that is, the truths of the Gospel)—his work will stand the test and will be unharmed by the fire. If he has used unworthy material in the building, his work will be consumed. He himself will be saved, but the destruction of his work will mean loss of reward.

Ministers of the Gospel are to be viewed by the church as instruments in God's hand. However, from God's view they are responsible persons, responsible to Him for the work they do.

The Holy Character of the Church (vv. 16-17). Paul reverted to the Corinthian believers, who, he reminded, were the temple of God. This referred to the entire church at Corinth. As well as dwelling in each Christian, the Spirit had made the whole church His home. Paul warned against violating the sanctity of God's dwelling place. "If any man defile [destroy] the temple of God, him shall God destroy" (v. 17).

Above Paul had spoken of putting inferior materials in the holy building, but here his thought shifted to the destruction of the

33

church. If false teachings were imported into the church or divisions developed among the members, the results could be devastating—destruction of both the offender and the church. It is not that the offender would be annihilated but his sin would be so grave that he would have rejected the possibility of salvation.

But can the church be destroyed? Matthew 16:18 teaches that "the gates of hell shall not prevail against [the Church]." It is well to remember that Paul had in view a local church, not the universal Church, and that heretical teachings have caused local churches to go out of existence. It is a serious matter to take part in anything that encourages a dividing and breaking up of the church.

THE CONCEPT OF CHRISTIAN MINISTERS AND THEIR WORK

Again Paul warned the Corinthians of worldly wisdom. Such wisdom was rooted and grounded in man. The Corinthians took pride in their cleverness and in their minsters to whom they attached themselves. So, in opposing all tendencies to worship the servants of God, the apostle expounded more on the Christian ministry.

Ministers (vv. 22-23). "Let no man glory in men" (v. 21). The Corinthians had done precisely the opposite. Respect for their ministers was proper, but they had gone beyond that, as their slogans reflect: "I belong to Paul; I belong to Apollos; I belong to Peter."

Paul inverted these slogans. Believers did not belong to this or that minister; but Paul, Apollos, and Peter belonged to them. Ministers are servants of Christ and thus belong to the church. All things belong to the believers. Why?

Christ is Lord of the world, life, death, and of this age and the age to come. Therefore, everything belongs to Christ. What is the Lord's is the Church's.[3] The members of each of the Corinthian

---

[3] Through Christ man recovers his lost lordship, but he will not recover it fully until Christ comes again.

factions had needlessly deprived themselves by exalting one minister while depreciating the others. Paul, Apollos, and Peter belonged to the Church. The best that each of them had to offer belonged to the Corinthians.

Servants and Stewards (4:1-5). Christ has chosen some to be His servants and stewards. The word *servant* used here means "an underoarsman." It emphasizes a subordinate position; that is, ministers are under the command of Christ who is the captain of the ship, the Church. A *steward* is "one who holds something in trust for another." As stewards, ministers have been entrusted by Christ with "the mysteries of God [the truths of the Gospel]" (v. 1) on which they are to nourish their people.

Since faithfulness is the chief virtue of a steward, God's judgment, not men's, determines whether a person stands or falls. For Paul, it was a matter of smallest importance to be critically examined by the Corinthians. He rejected any human attempt to do God's work. He had a good conscience, but he did not place any stock in it. "I [do not] judge . . . [my]self" (v. 3) His justification did not rest on a clear conscience but on God's grace. It is only God's grace that gives the Christian confidence.

The admonition "judge nothing before the time" (v. 5) condemns untimely verdicts. The thought turns to the Final Judgment when Christ returns. At that time He will throw a light on things hidden away in darkness and make known the good and bad thoughts of men and women. Then each person will receive praise.[4] Some of the Corinthians had praise for Paul; some, for Apollos; and some, for Peter. It was not for the Corinthians, but for God to give or withhold praise from the ministers. As at Corinth, the temptation among believers may be to leave God out and make man the measure of all things.

---

[4] At this point Paul did not say anything about those who will not receive praise. His concern was the Corinthian factions that made a practice of praising one of their ministers while condemning another.

Apostles (vv. 6-13). Among the believers at Corinth were those acting as if the kingdom of God had already fully come. They behaved as if trials and cross-bearing were past, as if Christ had already returned and they were reigning with Him, and enjoying resurrected life.

They were mistaken. The end had not yet come. So Paul ironically said, "I would to God ye did reign, that we also might reign with you" (v. 8).

At that time the apostles were not wearing crowns and were not seated on thrones. Before them constantly were the grim realities of sin, suffering, and death. They were like individuals on display in the arena just before perishing in combat with gladiators or beasts. They had become a spectacle of the whole universe, which included angels and men in its population (see Rom. 8:31-39).

Due to pride and the mistaken belief that they were reigning as kings, the Corinthians took the liberty to judge their ministers. Their party loyalties revealed condemnation of some and commendation of others. That was not their right, nor any man's, but only God's. Let "no one of you," wrote Paul, "be puffed up for one against another" (1 Cor. 4:6). No man has the right to boast of himself or of another. Whatever abilities he possesses he owes to God.

Pride had gripped the hearts of the Corinthians. They had forsaken the example of their ministers and had played them off against one another. The self-importance of the Corinthians stood in distinct contrast to the lifestyle of the apostles—men despised, abused, and treated as the scum of the earth.

Believers (vv. 14-21). Paul showed the concern of a genuine pastor for his people. His purpose was not to shame them but to admonish them as his "beloved sons" (v. 14). The church at Corinth had many teachers but only one spiritual father. That was Paul, who through the Gospel had begotten them to a new life from death in sin.

On the basis of his relation to his converts he made an appeal: "I beseech [beg] you [then], be ye followers [imitators] of me" (v. 16). The call was not to sporadic but to constant and habitual imitation. Paul had lived among them for months. His lifestyle had reflected Christ crucified and provided them with an immediate example. Their church problems would clear up if they were willing to become humble servants of Christ as Paul was.

Aware that they needed help, Paul promised to send Timothy, a trusted member of his staff and his spiritual child as the Corinthians were. The apostle said that Timothy would remind them of him. Their waywardness made it necessary for them to be instructed in the ways (behavior, doctrine) Paul had taught in all of the churches (7:17; 12:31; 14:33). Some of the puffed-up Corinthians had persuaded themselves that Paul would not dare set his foot in Corinth again. They might have said he was bold at a distance—in his letters—but afraid to appear personally. He warned them that he might come sooner than some thought "if the Lord wills" (4:19).

While the Holy Spirit does use human speech, the swelling words of the Corinthians were ineffective in bringing the kingdom of God. The Christian way of life stands on God's power that transforms the whole of life. Thus, in his appeal for unity, Paul declared that whether he came as a father who chastens his children or as a father who is proud of his children would depend on their response. Regardless of how he came, he would come in love. And at times love must be tough and wield the rod.

CONCLUSION

The trouble among the Corinthians and Paul's appeal for harmony are relevant now as then to the spiritual life of God's church. Factions that show their ugly heads in our churches often are caused by the exaltation of man rather than the exaltation of

Christ. The results are contentions, occupation with minor things rather than Biblical truth, and carnal cliques.

What a spectacle a strife-torn church is to a distressed world in desperate need of the saving message of Christ! But when the Spirit sweeps with His reviving power among God's people, the petty cliques and divisions vanish. As we get closer to Christ, we get closer to one another. Our personal preferences and opinions are adjusted so that the "unity of the Spirit" is maintained "in the bond of peace" (Eph. 4:3). Out utter obedience to Christ and submission to the indwelling Holy Spirit are seen the love that characterizes our fellowship.

As Paul, we are to exalt and praise Christ, the Church's one foundation and the source of Christian unity. We are to see our ministers as instruments of God's grace and hold them in high esteem. We do not fail to thank God for Bible-proclaiming, Christ-exalting, and example-setting ministers. Moreover, we remember that ministers are human also and need encouragement and understanding.

CHAPTER 3

A CALL FOR CHURCH DISCIPLINE
(5:1—6:20)

The problem of disunity demanded a great deal of attention. Paul turned to other disorders within the church. He had learned of a professing Christian who was living with his father's wife. Probably she was the man's stepmother. So he wrote to rebuke the Christians who saw nothing wrong with this relationship and to admonish stern discipline by excluding the immoral man from the church (ch. 5). On the other hand, some had yielded to the many invitations to visit the brothels and were ready to say, even in the case of fornication, "all things are lawful unto me" (6:12-20). They misused sex, one of the most sacred forces in the human personality and the basis of marriage, parenthood, and the family. Furthermore, some of the members of the church, having disagreements with other members, had brought their differences before pagan courts for settlement (vv. 1-11). Paul urged them to settle their petty disputes out of court with the counsel and the assistance of fellow believers.

It is true that the church at Corinth was in a moral atmosphere that was rotten to the core. That, however, did not provide an excuse for the Corinthians' insensitivity to sin in their midst nor for sin to be open and flagrant in the household of faith. While that small Christian community could not have been expected to change significantly that sex-saturated society, its members could maintain internal standards of purity and demonstrate the power of Christ by godly lives. Though the church was in a world where some, at the drop of a hat, went to law against their neighbor, its members should have settled their petty grievances among themselves rather than before unsaved judges.

At Corinth the church accepted sub-Christian standards and practices that were causing it to lose its power to witness to the unsaved and destroying its spiritual life. This becomes especially clear in view of the two problems—immorality and the habit of going to law—that were rather common among the Corinthian believers. Both of these deeply concerned Paul, and the way he dealt with them has deep theological implications for the Church today.

A CASE OF FORNICATION

Many of the converts among the Corinthians had not made a final break with their old lifestyles. Christ had called them out of vice and sin, but those who had not made a clean break were slipping back into their old pagan ways. Word had circulated that fornication had crept into the church. In the New Testament the word *fornication* is used for unchastity and illicit sexual relations of all kinds.

Here it is defined as one living with his father's wife; that is, with his stepmother. This is implied by Paul's choice of words— "his father's wife" rather than "his mother" (5:1). Paul did not call the relationship adultery or describe it as incest. Likely, the man's father had divorced the woman, or she was his father's widow.

The woman must have been unsaved, for Paul did not reprimand her or admonish the church to exclude her. Such gross immorality was forbidden among the Jews on the pain of death (Lev. 18:8; Deut. 22:30; 27:20). It was also not tolerated by Gentiles. Such a sin even caused pagans to blush, but it had entered into the church. Among the Corinthians there was no shame at such outrageous turpitude—a man having an affair with his stepmother.

Indifference of the Church (5:1-2). As incredible as that scandal was, the Corinthian believers were not disturbed. On the contrary, they were puffed up. This indicated more than just their pride about the fornicator in the church. They were proud that now they were spiritual persons and thought that they were beyond the restrictions of conventional religion. They regarded themselves as enlightened ones and assumed the old moral taboos had to give way to a new Christian freedom that allowed for fornication. If some disapproved of the new immorality, sheltered under pretext of Christian liberty, they probably were marked off as the unenlightened ones—the ones behind the times.

The circumstances did not call for arrogance but for mourning. Here the word for *mourning (pentheo)* is often used for grieving at a funeral. One among the Corinthians had died to God. A member of the church had been lost. That provided no occasion for arrogance but for mourning. Sin can and does creep into the church. It has no place there; but when sin is found among the redeemed, they must take it seriously. The church must purge itself of outrageous sin such as fornication reported among the Corinthians.

Judgment of the Offender (vv. 3-8). Sexual vice must not be tolerated by Christians. Immorality has no more place among Christians than does murder or larceny. Recognizing that, Paul pronounced judgement in the name and authority of Christ. He was physically absent but spiritually present. His absence from Corinth did not disqualify him as judge. Since the contrast was one between body and spirit, "present in spirit" (v. 3) indicates that in thought and concern Paul was at Corinth.

The apostle had already reached a verdict: hand the offender over to Satan. He went on to give the steps in taking disciplinary action: (1) The local church at Corinth was to meet "in the name of our Lord Jesus" (v. 4); that is, under His authority. (2) The church was to act with the assurance of Paul's support and influence. (3) "With the power of our Lord Jesus" (supernatural power granted to the church) the offender was to be removed from church membership. In the church Christ is Lord, but Satan exercises limited authority outside the church. To exclude the man from the sphere were Christ exercised His authority was to thrust him into the hands of Satan. Sin of such magnitude called for drastic action, but it was not to be vindictive.

There were two reasons for such discipline. The first was the man's spiritual welfare. Paul urged that he be handed over to Satan "for the destruction of the flesh, that [his] spirit may be saved in the day of the Lord Jesus" (v. 5).

The term *flesh* is significant. *Flesh* can be a synonym for "people" (Isa. 40:5). In the Old Testament, *flesh* particularly contrasts man's weakness with the strength of the Spirit (31:3). In Gethsemane, Jesus stressed it was due to weakness of the flesh that the disciples failed to watch and pray (Mark 14:38).

Flesh is not evil in itself, but under the influence of sin can and does become a source of moral evil. It provides a foothold for sin; it is the beachhead from which sin operates in human beings. Therefore, the handing of the man over to Satan was not to destroy his physical nature but his sinful lusts.

How can Satan have a purifying effect? The reverse might be expected (namely, a stimulation of sinful passions); but Scripture represents Satan as playing a disciplinary role in the experience of Job, as well as in Paul's recognition that his thorn in the flesh was a messenger of Satan to save him from being unduly elated (2 Cor. 12:7).

It is not that Paul was saying Satan was an evangelist and would try to save the man's soul, but Paul's hope was that thrusting the backslider out into the world where Satan reigned would cause him to become sick of the flesh-life and come to his senses. From his experience of the things of Satan, he would come to long for the things of God. Being buffeted by Satan, he would repent and return to the fellowship of the church. At the Final Judgment, Paul expected him to be among the redeemed. Thus, the drastic remedy would benefit the patient.

The second reason for the disciplinary measure was the purity of the church. The sin of the immoral can spread like an infection throughout the body of Christ and defile the entire Church.

To make this clear, Paul used the illustration of the Feast of the Passover and specifically leaven, which, in Scripture, represents sin. A strict Jew made a careful search for every scrap of leaven in his home so that it could be cast out before the celebration of the Passover began. For the next seven days, the Feast of Unleavened Bread, no leaven was used or kept in the home.

Sin works in the Church as does leaven in dough. By being puffed up, the Corinthians revealed that the moral infection had spread. Just as a small amount of leaven can permeate a whole lump of dough, the sin of one member can corrupt the whole life of a church and mar its holiness. Fornication is a sin against the Church.

The Church must exercise discipline to preserve its purity. "Purge out therefore the old leaven, that ye may be a new lump" (1 Cor. 5:7). This command assumes what God did in Christ to save us from sin. The Passover Feast celebrated Israel's deliverance from Egypt. Paul declared that Christ is our Passover Lamb, who has already been sacrificed.

According to Jewish practice, leaven was disposed before observing the feast. But God has provided for us the Lamb of sacrifice beforehand. Christians do not need to wait for special seasons of the year to remember what God has done. Our new life begins when we believe on Christ and the leaven of sin is removed from our hearts.

There follows, in a spiritual sense, a Feast of Unleavened

Bread—a walk that avoids the leaven of sin and a life that reflects obedience to Christ. Such is not temporary but permanent on the part of those redeemed. Literally, Paul's admonition was, "Let us keep on observing the feast." Christians are to live in the festival founded by Christ. That consists of living with no trace of the leaven of the old life and of thanking God for His mighty deliverance from the bondage of sin.

Sadly to say, malice and wickedness remained in the household of faith at Corinth. To protect its purity, the church needed to remove the sinful member and replace malice and wickedness by sincerity and truth.

Agreement With a Previous Letter (vv. 9-13). Paul had already written about the grave matter of keeping company with immoral people in the church. The Corinthians had interpreted his instructions to mean that all contact with sinners was to be avoided. That was a misunderstanding and would have made it necessary for the Christians to withdraw from life completely and live in solitude. They could have had nothing to do with the unsaved—nothing to do with the pagan society about them.

That was not what Paul had in mind in his first letter. Apparently the Corinthians excused themselves from any serious attempt to deal with sin in the church because they reasoned that they could live entirely separated from it outside the church. Paul's concern was sinners in the church. So he explained that any man who bore the name of *Christian* (literally, "being named a brother"), but was immoral, greedy, worshiped idols, or was a slanderer, a drunkard, or thief was not to be included in the church's fellowship.

The conduct of such a one revealed that he was a Christian no longer. The believers were not to eat with such a person at the Lord's Table or at any other occasion. Socially embracing a grossly immoral person within the church did nothing to influence him to break with his loose living; however it did taint the holy character of the church and undermine its high moral standards.

Christians mixing with immoral people who are outside the Church is one thing, but with those who are in the Church is another. Christians are not to withdraw from common life and isolate themselves from the unsaved of low morals. Jesus did not. He ate with publicans and sinners (Mark 2:15). Socially He was free, but He did not deny His prophetic freedom to declare God's sure judgment of the ungodly. Social freedom and the purity of the Church are two different matters. Should a Christian fall into open sin and persist in it, as did the fornicator at Corinth, for his sake and for the sake of the Church he should be excluded from the fellowship of the church.

Therefore, as Paul advised, a church is not to judge the outsiders but those within its own ranks. It is the responsibility of the local church to judge its own members. God will judge the unsaved; they are to be left in His hands. At the Final Judgment, believers will judge the world (1 Cor4. 6:2).

In chapter 6, Paul's concern was not the Final Judgment but the spiritual and moral condition of the Church. The Church is held responsible and is called to act promptly to remove reproach from its midst. In the household of faith, judgment is directed inward and must exclude from Christian fellowship those guilty of practicing flagrant, open sin.

If such is tolerated and not judged, the Church will suffer. Its worship of God will decline; its enthusiasm for high spiritual standards will wane; its testimony will be damaged; its power will diminish. In view of such devastating results, again Paul insisted that the sinful member, the fornicator, be excluded from the local church fellowship.

MISUSE OF THE BODY

It is unthinkable that Christians would assume they could give themselves to lustful relationships with the opposite sex. But the fatal disease of fornication had spread among the believers at Corinth. More were guilty than the man having an affair with his stepmother. Some were acquiring the Greek attitude toward the body. The Greeks had contempt for the body. For them, what man did with his body was insignificant. Supposing the body was insignificant, the Corinthian believers thought they were at liberty to commit fornication. So, over against this pagan notion, Paul introduced the Christian view of the body.

The Sanctity of the Body (vv. 12-18). Men in the Corinthian Church pushed the doctrine of Christian liberty so far as to make it mean that the believer had the right to do whatever he wished. Self-indulgence was practiced on the grounds that Christian freedom was license. Especially is this reflected in their slogans, one of which was "All things are lawful." Paul corrected this evil imagination: "All things are not expedient [helpful, profitable]" (v. 12).

Things may be lawful for Christians to do, but they may not be helpful for others and for themselves. Driving a car is not wrong in itself, but driving it carelessly or on the wrong side of the road is. That would endanger the lives of others as well as the driver. Christians, therefore, should be careful about their actions so that what they do serves the welfare of others. They must exercise discernment in the use of freedom. To put it another way, they are to prove "what is that good, and acceptable, and perfect, will of God" (Rom. 12:2). Their actions must be not only lawful but responsible and helpful.

What some of the Corinthians were doing was unlawful and irresponsible. They fancied themselves to be free to have dealings with harlots, but Paul reminded them that he "will not be brought under the power of any." The word *any* can refer to anyone of the "all things" (1 Cor. 6:12). Paul would not allow himself to become a slave to anyone of the things that were "lawful." A Corinthian who had placed his body at the disposal of a harlot had brought himself under her authority. More than that, he had come under the power of his own inexpedient practices and lustful desires.

Even things that may be lawful may enslave us. For example, food and drink are necessary; but if we gorge ourselves, we may become a slave to our appetites. Enslavement results from abuse. The believer should not be brought under the power of anything, especially not sensuality. Desires are natural enough, but the Lord enables us not to be controlled by any of them.

Another Corinthian slogan was, "Meats are for the belly, and the belly for the meats." That was right. Whatever is eaten is broken down and digested in the stomach. God has ordained it. There is nothing wrong with a Christian eating and satisfying his appetite.

But the Corinthians had drawn the wrong conclusion: since the stomach was made for food, the body (in particular, the sex organs) must have been made for fornication. Properly understood, sexual relations are not merely satisfying an appetite like eating food. The body should not be confused with the stomach.

Here the term *body* refers to more than flesh and blood; it is man's personality—not just one part, but man as a whole. His body and personality cannot be separated. Each exerts a vital influence on the other. When I dedicated myself to Christ, I committed my body and personality to Him. "Your bodies" in Romans 12:1 is equivalent to "yourselves."

The point is that the sexual act is an act of the whole person. It is the sharing of one's total self as nearly as one can with another person. It is a union of personalities. Through sexual union, a man and a woman are united in the most intimate bond. As Genesis 2:24 says, "[The two] shall be[come] one flesh."

The body was meant to be an instrument for the service and honor of the Lord, not for fornication. Therefore, the Corinthian idea that the body was meant for fornication was wrong. The proper view is that the body is intended for the Lord and the Lord for the body (or the whole person).

In fact, the body is ultimately meant for redemption. Christ died to redeem the whole man. He became flesh and took on a body such as ours that He might redeem our mortal body. The body will not pass away; it will be changed and raised up. God, who raised up the Lord, will raise us up by His glorious power (Rom. 8:23; 1 Cor. 15:51-53).

Honor will be done to our bodies when they are raised. At the Last Day everyone will receive what he deserves, according to what he has done in his body, whether good or bad (2 Cor. 5:10). The bodies of Christians are intended for the Lord's service; they will ultimately be fashioned like unto His glorious body. Sex outside of marriage defiles the person. By going to prostitutes the Corinthians defiled themselves and sinned against the doctrine of the resurrection of believers.

Paul appealed to the Corinthians' common knowledge: "Know ye not that your bodies are the members of Christ?" (1 Cor. 6:15). The tragedy was not that they did not have knowledge, but (like Christians so often today), they did not use what they had.

They knew that through faith in Christ the believer is united with Christ, and the whole man becomes a member of Christ. Each of them had been joined to Christ by the Spirit of God. Christ had dignified them to the last degree by taking them into union with Himself; and God had honored them by designing them for resurrection.

Sad to say, the Corinthians had handed over the members of Christ to prostitutes. By visiting the brothels, they had transferred the members from Christ to harlots; that is, they had given themselves to harlots, thereby dishonoring what was intended for the Resurrection and denying Christ the use of what was entirely His own. Their unholy alliances with harlots had destroyed their union with Christ.

Sexual relations outside of marriage are sin against the Church and the Resurrection. Moreover, they are sin against the total personality, which Paul called the "body." They have a profound affect on the root and the whole of the human personality.

There are other sins against the body—gluttony, drunkenness, and so on. But neither the food devoured by a glutton nor the wine consumed by a drunkard defiles one as does fornication. None of these stain more and have longer lasting consequences than sexual irregularities. The one who commits fornication sins not only against God and the other person involved but against his own body. At Corinth members of the church had given their bodies (themselves), which rightly belonged to the Lord, to harlots.

The apostle urged the practice of fleeing from immorality. Fornication begets a multitude of evils well known to us all. It defiles the Church and destroys homes and corrupts society. But when this hideous sin shows its head within the precincts of the Church, the results are nothing less than tragic.

Reasons for Clean Living (vv. 19-20). (1) As Christians, our bodies, our whole selves, are the dwelling place of the Holy Spirit. In 3:16, Paul referred to the community of believers as the temple of the Spirit, but here he pointed out that the Holy Spirit dwells in each Christian. As God dwelt in the Tabernacle and Temple, in His Shekinah glory, so He dwells in His people by the Holy Spirit.

Each Christian is a place where God dwells. He is a temple of the Holy Spirit. Therefore, he must keep the temple pure, lest the divine Guest depart. All that is unworthy of the heavenly Guest— drinking, drugs, immorality, and other unclear habits—have no place in the life of the child of God. Such grieve the Holy Spirit and defile His dwelling place. Every precaution must be taken to ensure that He enjoys a clean temple.

(2) The believer is not his own. Why? Paul's answer was "Ye are bought with a price." The Greek for *bought (agorazo)* meant "to frequent the marketplace," and thus implied "to purchase, to buy." *Price (time)* was "a value by which the price is fixed." Christ has purchased or redeemed us by payment of His own precious blood. He has made us His own (1 Peter 1:18-19). But at what a price!

The greatness of this price tells us of man's dignity and worth. Man appears weak and insignificant, but there is no doubt of his essential value in light of the ransom paid for his redemption. His real worth is seen only at Calvary. Christ died for the whole man to redeem him from bondage.

The blacklist of sins—fornication, idolatry, adultery, theft, drunkenness, slander, swindling (1 Cor. 6:9-10)—remind us, as well as the Corinthians, that Christ has delivered us from such. Therefore, since we are His possessions and are indwelt by the Holy Spirit, we are to glorify God in our whole being—body and spirit—by chastity and holy living, and by devotion and praise.

LAWSUITS BEFORE UNSAVED JUDGES

As we have seen, the Corinthians had been careless about gross sin in their midst. But, on the other hand, some had been sensitive about their own personal rights and had gone to court against members of the congregation. This had spread an atmosphere of contention. So Paul called for them to settle their disputes over trivial matters within the church rather than in civil court. There are two reasons Paul advised them not to use the courts for lawsuits.

Denies the Dignity of the Christian (vv. 1-6). The Corinthians went to court before "the unjust" (*hoi adikoi*, literally "the unrighteous"). This does not mean the judges in the courts were "unjust" in their judgments. The Roman legal system was noted for its justice. Rather, the term "unrighteous" refers to the fact that they were unsaved and therefore not justified and rightly related to Christ.

Before unbelievers the Corinthians washed their dirty linen. Paul was against this practice for several reasons:

(1) In the Final Judgment Christians (*hagioi*, "saints") will judge the world. If they are able to judge both men and angels in God's final court, they must be competent to deal with their own petty disputes.

(2) Christians should not settle their disputes before those "who are least esteemed in the church" (v. 4). That was exactly what the Corinthians had attempted. They had turned to unsaved judges who had legal training but who judged by the world's standards and had no standing in the church.

(3) Among Christians should be a wise man, one capable of acting as judge. The Corinthians had boasted about wisdom. It would have been better to have a wise Christian among them to decide between two brothers. The practice of brother going to law against brother before unbelievers reflected on the dignity and personal integrity of the Christians. A church is in sad condition when Christians think they are more likely to get justice from unbelievers than from their brothers in the Lord!

Denies the Reality of the Christian Experience (vv. 7-11). Among the Corinthians, strife in the household of faith was made a public spectacle in the courts. Paul wrote that their legal disputes showed "there is utterly a fault among you" (v. 7) or "you have completely failed." Their moral failure was obvious. Brother suing brother had dishonored Christ and encouraged strife in the church.

Rather than demanding their personal rights, a hard but better course of action would have been for them to bear injury (v. 7). Jesus, as well as Paul, taught it is far better to suffer evil than to do evil (Matt. 5:39-42). The Corinthians who were always running to court were not seeking justice but were trying to defraud one another. They had done injury to one another and to the cause of Christ.

It is well to note that Paul did not forbid a Christian to use court of law to secure justice. What he condemned was the habitual practice of going to court over trivial matters. Because of Jewish injustice, Paul himself appealed to Caesar, the highest court of that day (Acts 25:10-11). The reference in 1 Corinthians 6 was not to serious suits, but to petty quibbles.

What the Corinthians were doing could have had fatal results. In so many words, Paul advised, "Make no mistake: the immoral, the greedy, and the unscrupulous will have no part in the kingdom of God." That was plain talk to a city like Corinth. And it is needed today as much as it was then.

Once the Corinthian believers had been among the most notorious transgressors. Some of them had been fornicators, idolaters, adulterers, effeminate, homosexual perverts; others had been thieves, covetous, drunkards, revilers, and extortioners. Among them was a good assortment of former immoral and criminal persons. They had practiced vile things of the flesh, sins that were quite common in Corinth.

Now they were changed. They were spiritually washed, sanctified, and justified. They were saved by grace alone. What God's matchless grace had done for them! Rescued from the slime of a sinful past, they needed to magnify God's grace. They needed to turn from their old sinful ways and behave as brothers and sisters in Christ.

Like the Corinthians, every believer must measure up to God's standard of holiness. Why does God demand that we cease from sin, turn from every filthy habit and vile passion, and glorify Christ? We are God's. We are indwelt by the Holy Spirit. Let us seek to please not ourselves, but our Owner and heavenly Guest, the Holy Spirit. To do that we cannot run our lives as we please, but only as God wills (Eph. 4:30-32).

CONCLUSION

Serious sin and disputes among the people of God call for church discipline today. Sin is contagious. For this reason, the Church cannot afford to be careless about sin in its midst. As well as contaminating the Church, open sin among God's people does damage to its witness in a world perishing without the Gospel. If Christians are no different from unbelievers, how can they claim that Christ has power to transform life? They may preach that Christ has such power, but by their conduct actually deny it.

To protect its purity and the power and influence of its witness, the Church must discipline itself. Discipline is never vindictive nor merely punitive but redemptive. The purity of the Church must be maintained. Open sin has to be purged; otherwise it works like leaven in a lump of dough.

Discipline always must be administered with care and love so that no one is excluded for the wrong reasons or in the wrong way. Discipline improperly exercised or applied in the wrong spirit creates strife and division among believers. The importance of dealing with an erring member with care and love cannot be overstated. When circumstances seem to merit disciplinary action, it may be well for us to ponder what Wagner suggests:

> In the first place there must be no doubt of sin really being committed. Discipline cannot be based on rumors; it must be undergirded by solid fact. . . . Second, the moral problem in question must be recognized as sin before anyone can be disciplined for it. There should be no question about

fornication in anyone's mind. . . . [The] church must decide for itself where to draw the line between prohibition and permission. Finally, sin which precipitates excommunication must be a measurable sin. Some definite sins are quite unmeasurable and therefore almost impossible to judge. If you try open discipline for such subjective things as envy, hypocrisy, bitterness, or lack of love, you are in for a difficult time. Without doubt these are some of the most destructive sins in the Church, but ordinarily they fall outside the limits of discipline. They must be left to God.[1]

On the other hand, the disputes among the Corinthians also disrupted the fellowship of the church and damaged its testimony. Disputes might not have called for as drastic remedy as did immoral conduct, but wrangling and strife among the brethren gave evidence of spiritual immaturity. The cure for disputes was not demanding one's rights—some of the Corinthians had already tried that in court. And what they did spread an atmosphere of contention.

Aware of that, Paul asked the believers at Corinth: "Why do ye not rather take wrong? Why do ye not rather suffer yourselves to be defrauded?" (1 Cor. 6:7). It is not right for a Christian to insist on his personal rights, especially when this may injure the cause of Christ; but it is right for him to suffer wrong when this is done for the common welfare of the church (cf. 1 Peter 2:13—4:19).

To have a dispute at all is a defeat. There are no winners, even if the right party wins. Indeed, such encourages strife and hatred in the Christian fellowship and brings a reproach on Christ if the world becomes aware of wranglings among Christians. The inspired wisdom of Paul counsels us that the real cure for disputes within the church is meekness and unselfishness on the part of those who suffer wrong.

---

[1] C. Peter Wagner, *A Turned-On Church in an Uptight World*, pp. 53-54.

CHAPTER 4

THE CHRISTIAN VIEW OF SEX AND MARRIAGE
(7:1-40)

Marriage as an institution ordained by God was understood and appreciated by Paul. His letters—especially Ephesians, Colossians, and 1 and 2 Timothy—offer specific instructions on the marriage relationship. Too, they make clear his high view of the sacredness of marriage and his keen insight into the marriage relationship.

Among the believers at Corinth were some who belittled marriage. They were ascetics who insisted that a Christian should give no place to marriage and sex. Anything that had to do with the instincts and desires of the body was thought to be evil and was to be completely suppressed.

This was precisely the opposite of those at Corinth who believed that what they did with the body was unimportant. As we have seen, these gave full range to their natural appetites by lying with harlots.

This makes it clear that there were two views of sex and marriage among the Corinthians. One was that what a person does with the body is inconsequential and that sex outside of marriage is all right. The other was that sex is dirty and a Christian, even if married, should not indulge in physical relations.[1] Strange as it may seem,

---

[1] *Libertinism* and *asceticism* are the technical terms to describe the two views. Libertinism holds the physical body in contempt by discounting the fact that what is done

the two views, though opposite as they are, emerged from the tendency to despise the body and see bodily desires as sinful. What lies behind 1 Corinthians 7 is the second view: the body is evil; therefore natural desires must be totally suppressed by Christians, even to the point of denying the most intimate act of the marriage relationship. Paul would have nothing of this unchristian view. For him the natural needs are God-given to serve high and holy purposes. Contrary to what the Corinthians, at least some of them, had begun to teach, marriage is holy. Sex is the basis of the most intimate relationship in life between husband and wife; it is also intended for the perpetuity of the race.

Regretfully, chapter 7 of 1 Corinthians has been misunderstood. It is well to remember that the section does not give a systematic exposition of the Christian doctrine of marriage, but Paul's answer to specific questions put to him in a letter, apparently by a group of ascetics in the church. Chapter 7 deals with the subject of sex and marriage in general, and it answers the questions pertaining to local problems in an extremely practical manner. Paul affirmed (1) the legitimacy of marriage, (2) the legitimacy of sexuality in marriage, (3) equal rights and responsibilities within sex and marriage, and (4) the practical advantages of the single state for pioneer evangelists.

CHRISTIAN MARRIAGE

No human relationship is more noble than marriage, but it has been popular to think that Paul had a rather negative attitude toward matrimony. To give credence to such a view, not a few have cited the words: "It is good for a man not to touch a woman" (7:1). This may well be one of the slogans of the Corinthian Church rather

---

in the body can contaminate the whole person. Asceticism, however, takes seriously the danger of contamination and is motivated by fear as well as a low view of the body. It seems odd that two such extremes should meet in the same place, but in light of 1 Corinthians they apparently did.

than Paul's own view.[2] Probably Paul was quoting a passage from the Corinthian letter to him, for he sharply qualified the slogan.

Marriage Is Proper (v. 2). It should be noted that for Paul the norm was *monogamy*—a man and woman living together until death severs the marriage bond. Each man is to have a wife; and each woman, a husband. Marriage is wise. Among other things, it acts as protection against fornication. Men and women have sexual desires. These are proper, but the unmarried may run the risk of being tempted to sexual impurity. Normal sexual desires can find proper fulfillment in the institution of marriage, which God himself appointed.

Did Paul here take a low view of marriage—"to avoid fornication" (v. 2)? We would do well to remember where his readers were. They were in Corinth—a city where they were constantly facing temptation. Fornication was so prevalent that it was not considered serious sin. Temptation was lurching at them on every hand. The advice that it was better to marry than to fall into sin may appear to have put marriage on a low basis. The truth is that Paul faced squarely the facts by recognizing the lightness with which fornication was held in Corinth and the fact the Corinthian believers, like other people, had normal desires and appetites.

In offering some practical counsel, Paul set forth a rule that is universally true—no Christian should attempt an unnatural lifestyle. Each should choose a way of life in which he can best live the Christian life. No one should deliberately surround himself with temptation. If he does, he is asking for "scandal."

---

[2] If it represents Paul's own view, the statement affirms simply the legitimacy of the single state, but does not elevate it over the married state. Paul said that "it is good," rather than "it is better" for a man to remain single. We may feel that it is good for a man to devote himself to the Christian ministry, however, with no thought that there is anything improper about serving the church in another capacity. Likely, "It is good for a man not to touch a woman" was a slogan of an ascetic group at Corinth. Compare it with Genesis 2:18: "It is not good that the man should be alone."

Every Christian should determine what his own needs are and choose the lifestyle in which he can best render service and devotion to the Lord. An unnatural way of life breeds unhappiness, and can have disastrous consequences.

Under God, both the single and wedded state are honorable. One is not superior to the other. Paul's incisive understanding of this matter is reflected by his belief that different people have different gifts and that each should order his or her life according to the gift that God has granted. He regarded his own unmarried state as a gift of God (v. 9).

Christianity does not call anyone to deny his humanity. While the self-discipline and purity of the unmarried are to be admired, it must be remembered that it is no part of Christian duty to suppress the natural passions that find their proper satisfaction with marriage. Each is called to order his life according to the divine order. The divine intent is to sanctify man's natural desires and to channel them to the greater glory of God.

Partners Have Mutual Rights and Responsibilities (vv. 3-7). True marriage involves responsibilities as well as joys. Husband and wife are not to live as though they are unmarried. They are to render to one another "due benevolence" (v. 3), which means a man should fulfill his duty as a husband and a woman should fulfill her duty as a wife.

The husband has "power" (*exousiazo,* "authority") over his wife, and vice versa. By entering into holy matrimony, man and woman imply that they are giving up exclusive rights to their bodies, agreeing to share them fully with one another.

Among the Corinthians were those convinced that marriage should involve only spiritual but not physical love. But when one partner spiritualizes the relationship, the other is "robbed" (King James Version, "defrauded") of his or her rights. The Scriptural view is that physical and spiritual cannot be separated, not even in language, for the Biblical word for sexual intercourse means "to know."

The most fulfilling marriages are characterized by spiritual affection and loyalty in which each partner seeks the physical satisfaction of the other. Under these conditions, the husband never regards his wife merely as a means of self-gratification, but he keeps in focus the whole relationship—the spiritual and the physical—in which they both experience satisfaction of all their desires.

Some of the Corinthians had a distorted picture of sex. They thought Christian couples should separate and not live together as man and wife. While sex in marriage does not make prayer impossible or improper, it is in order for a couple, by mutual consent, to abstain a limited time for spiritual retreat. But then they should return to the normal marital relations. Otherwise, they open the door to Satan's tempting them to satisfy their desires in fornication. The idea that sex is bad has wrecked many marriages, and apparently it was doing that very thing at Corinth.

There is no doubt that Paul taught the sanctity of sex, but two of his statements that follow have been quite puzzling: (1) "I speak this by permission [*sunggnome*, 'concession'], and not of commandment" (v. 6). Probably this refers to verse 5 where Paul advised husbands and wives not to rob one another of their rights.[3] His concession was to couples who agreed not to cohabit for a short time so that they might give themselves to prayer and fasting without distractions. This was not by "command," but he conceded that it was proper. (2) "I would [*thelo*, 'wish, desire'] that all men were even as I myself" (v. 7). Is then celibacy, living without marriage, morally superior? What Paul desired for all people was not mere celibacy but freedom from sexual impurity and obedience to God. This can be fulfilled in more ways than

---

[3] Some scholars have connected verse 6 with verses 2-5, which recommend marriage. If so, Paul said he was not commanding anyone to marry, but conceded that each may have a wife.

one. Each person has his or her own gift. Paul's point was that some have the gift to remain single and serve God best in that condition. On the other hand, he advised those who lacked it to marry, for to them God had granted other special gifts. Marriage certainly is not sinful and not second-best.

CELIBACY

Living without marriage, as we have observed, has no moral advantage. Under certain conditions it may have practical advantages. Like Paul, many pioneer ministers and missionaries have found that the single state allows them to devote themselves to the service of the Lord with no distractions. Jesus himself taught that there is a place in the kingdom of God for the unmarried (Matt. 19:12).

The apostle's own personal preference was to remain single.[4] The reason was not that he considered marriage inferior, but that he might devote himself to the ministry of the Gospel free of the responsibilities of a family. He advised the unmarried and those who had lost their partners by death to remain as they were. His concern was entirely practical:

> I would have you without carefulness [anxiety, worry]. He that is unmarried careth for the things that belong to the Lord. . . . But he that is married careth for the things that are of the world, how he may please his wife. . . . The unmarried woman careth for the things of the Lord, that she may be holy both in body and in spirit: but she that is married careth for the things of the world, how she may please her husband (7:32-34).

---

[4] At this time Paul did not have a wife. While it is possible that he had never been married, it is probable that he was a widower. Unmarried rabbis were rare. Some have assumed that he was a member of the Sanhedrin and that this rules out any doubt that he was once married. This poses two problems: (1) We do not know whether he was a member of the Sanhedrin. (2) In the fourth century, only married men could be members of that court. It is not known that this was the case in the first century.

Married men's and women's interests are divided. If each took no thought of their companion, they would be unfaithful to their marriage vows. Each spouse has solemn responsibilities to their partner.

The misfortune is not that married persons are married, but that they are torn between the world's affairs and the Lord's affairs. Paul said the unmarried woman cares about the things of the Lord "that she may be holy both in body and in spirit."[5] Did he mean that the unmarried state is morally superior and that the unmarried woman is able to sanctify her body since she has no husband? Not at all, for such an idea is incongruent with Paul's insistence on the purity of the marriage bond.

Too, Paul taught that all Christians must be holy in body (Rom. 6:12; 12:1; 1 Cor. 6:13, 15, 19). "That she may be holy both in body and in spirit" may be a Corinthian slogan, especially that of the ascetics. Paul approved of holiness for all Christians—married and unmarried. The married, as well as the unmarried, are to be holy in body and in spirit.

It is not that married life cannot be consecrated, nor that the unmarried can achieve a higher level of holiness. However, marriage does introduce new cares. Those who have families know their time is consumed by such everyday matters as caring for the children and home, shopping, and keeping the budget balanced. If the unmarried remain as they are, they will have fewer obligations and can give their undivided attention to the Lord.

This is not a rule: "Not that I may cast a snare upon you"; or, better rendered, "not in order to put a halter around your necks" (1 Cor. 7:35). If the unmarried cannot exercise self-control, it is better for them to marry than to be consumed by unchaste

---

[5] It is difficult to decide in verse 34 if a distinction is intended between the "unmarried woman" (*agamos*) and the "virgin" (*parthenos*). An unmarried woman might be a virgin. Perhaps Paul had in mind only one group and used "virgin" as an explanation of "unmarried."

desire (v. 9). The reason should be clear: marriage is honorable (Heb. 13:4), and lust is sinful (Matt. 5:28). Tortured by passion, a Christian cannot wait on the Lord without distraction.

No one course of action holds for every individual. Marriage and family responsibilities are God's will for the majority of human beings. However, some can live full, pure, and honorable lives outside of marriage. "Every man hath his proper gift of God, one after this manner, and another after that" (1 Cor. 7:7). Each must fashion his life according to the gift that God has given and avoid pursuing a lifestyle for which he is ill-suited.

PERMANENCE OF MARRIAGE

Marriage is a lifetime partnership. Apparently, some of the new converts at Corinth were not committed to the permanence of this relationship. They were breaking up their marriages and homes. The apostle turned to those who felt that they no longer needed marriage.

While Paul granted that the unmarried may marry, he forbade divorce. A husband should not divorce his wife, and she should not separate from her husband. This charge Paul gave on the authority of the Lord (Mark 10:2-12). Christians are bound by the teaching of Jesus. If separation seems the only solution, the woman should remain single or make up with her husband. Leaving him must not be used as a stepping-stone to a second marriage.

Paul gave no similar advice to the husband who divorces his wife. The implication is that he should do likewise; that is, remain unmarried or return to his wife. Those that are bound to a wife are not to seek to be free (1 Cor. 7:27). A wife is bound as long as her husband is alive (v. 39). The husband is equally bound. If a woman's husband "falls asleep" (dies), she is free to marry whom she wishes; presumably the husband is permitted to remarry if his wife dies. Paul qualified this, however, with the words "only in the Lord" (v. 39)—sound advice for anyone contemplating marriage. The widow can marry whomever she desires, provided he is a Christian. She is wise to choose a Christian husband, but the apostle expressed the opinion that she will be happier if she remains single. Marriage brings added responsibilities.

MIXED MARRIAGES

In the community of believers at Corinth, there were marriages that involved only one Christian. Such a situation had come into being through the conversion of one of the partners rather than a Christian marrying an unbeliever. Paul had spoken to Christian couples, but here he turned to Christian husbands with non-Christian wives and to Christian wives with non-Christian husbands. Christ did not speak on this matter; thus Paul conceded that he did not have a direct command regarding marriages where only one spouse was a Christian. Yet, his charge concerning mixed marriages does not have less authority than his charge of verse 10. Paul spoke as a divinely inspired apostle (v. 40).

Unbroken by the Believer (vv. 12-14). The Christian, whether husband or wife, is not to initiate divorce. Likely, some at Corinth said that no believer should live with an unbeliever. But Paul advised against dividing marriages and homes. If the unbeliever is content to live with the believer, the marriage should remain unimpaired.

Keeping the marriage together serves the interest of peace, the home, and the couple; but more specifically, the unbeliever is sanctified by the believer, and the children are clean. This does not mean the faith of a Christian saves the other members of the family. The apostle did not use the verb *sanctify* (*hagiazein*) with its customary meaning.

The clue to this may be found in the Corinthian situation. As already observed, some were opposed generally to marriage and sex. However, others felt that marriage between Christians was proper, but mixed marriages should be forbidden. For the believer would be defiled by the unbeliever and the children born to the union would be unclean.

On the contrary, the Christian has a sanctifying influence on the marriage and the unbelieving companion. The children born to the union are also holy. The entire family is brought under the sanctifying influence of the Gospel.

There are certain spiritual benefits that unbelievers derive through their fellowship with believers. Christianity is a source of blessing in any home and should become the dominating influence in the family, even if only one parent is a believer. The faith of one parent affects the life of the whole household.

Broken by the Unbeliever (v. 15). If the unbeliever does not want to continue the marriage, what should the Christian do? Paul said, "A brother or a sister is not under bondage in such cases." The Christian is not enslaved. If the unbeliever's heart has become so hardened that he or she desires separation, the Christian spouse (as a last resort) should let the marriage break up.

Does this mean the deserted believer is allowed to remarry? What is the meaning of "not under bondage" (*ou dedoulotai;* literally, "is not enslaved")? It could mean either "is not bound to live with an unbeliever" or "is not obligated to the marriage bond," therefore free to remarry. The scholars who follow the latter interpretation call this "the Pauline privilege." It really is not clear what is meant by "not under bondage." The question of remarriage is not raised in verses 12-16.

In a mixed marriage where the unsaved one absolutely refuses to live with the Christian, Paul's advice is let the unbeliever separate. God calls the Christian to peace. The unbeliever may be so strongly antagonistic to the Christian faith that he or she ridicules and persecutes the believer to the point that there is no home left. For the sake of the peace of the home and the well-being of the children, it is better to separate than to stay and fight, attempting to maintain what is only the semblance of a family. The Christian has not been called to war but peace.[6]

Evangelization at Home (v. 16). Only as a last resort is a mixed marriage to be dissolved. The unsaved partner may, in time, be saved. Rather than shedding their companions, Christians married to unbelievers should seek to win them to the Savior. This can best be done not by preaching sermons, which can easily be construed as nagging, but by love and patience.

As stated above, in a mixed marriage the unbeliever is brought under the sanctifying influence of Christian marriage. Vital to this is the quality of life that the believer lives and provides in the home. A Christian wife can best bring her husband to accepting her faith by consistent living and providing him with a happy home.

However, Paul's concern for the believer's converting the unsaved partner provides no ground for Christians marrying non-Christians with the hope of winning them over. That Paul advised widows to remarry "only in the Lord" strongly implies that he would have condemned such.

THE UNMARRIED AND THE ENGAGED

Paul, we have seen, enunciated the duties of the married. His approval of marriage is shown by his prohibition of divorce. To the unmarried he had no charge from the Lord, but he offered his inspired counsel on the matter.

Again, in verse 26, the apostle said it was good for a man to remain single. This was because of "the present distress" (*ten enestosan anagken* or "the present necessity"). What "the present necessity" was we are not certain. Some have suggested it was the

---

[6] Another way of taking this is that a Christian should not dissolve the marriage on religious grounds. Such would create strife.

troubles to precede the second coming of Christ, but Paul did not ordinarily speak of these events as a necessity.

He was probably referring to local conditions in Corinth, such as social and political unrest and persecution. The Corinthian believers were living in difficult times; they already had enough troubles. So why should they add to them by seeking marriage with its responsibilities? On the other hand, the married were not to seek release from marriage. Whether married or unmarried, everyone was to remain as they were.

Against the tendency at Corinth to despise marriage, Paul said that if one married, he had not sinned. Too, if a virgin (a young unmarried girl) married, she had committed no sin. Men and women were free to marry; but if they did, they would expose themselves to the "trouble in the flesh" (v. 28) or the responsibilities that go with marriage. Those tempted to rush into this relationship were to weigh carefully the added burden of married life.

The Christian must not allow himself to become engrossed in worldly interests. Because of the conditions existing at that time, Paul said, "The time is short" (v. 29). Many take this as a reference to the second advent of Christ; but apparently it refers to circumstances at Corinth. These might have been similar to conditions that will exist before the End.[7]

Verse 31 provides direction in understanding this: "the fashion [*schema*, 'form'] of this world passeth [is passing] away"; that is, the social and commercial institutions in their present form will not last too much longer. The husband should realize that although the institution of marriage shapes his life, it is passing away. There is so little time to live and to serve Christ.

---

[7] The important feature of 1 Corinthians 7:26-31 is not the nearness of the End, but its certainty. The End-time started with the first coming of Christ, but it will be consummated when He comes again. At Pentecost, Peter reminded this audience that the outpouring of the Holy Spirit was a sign of the End-time. Since that time, we have lived "in the last days" (Acts 2:17).

The husband should begin to prepare for heaven, but not by divorcing his wife or by becoming a celibate and ceasing to enjoy her fellowship. Rather, he should be devoted to the Lord as if he had no wife to distract him.

Paul's purpose was not to restrain married relationships nor to hint that men should neglect their wives, chasing around with other women as though they had none. His desire was that marriage partners reflect an undivided devotion to the Lord.

Those who weep and rejoice, who buy and use the world, should live as though they did none of these. This does not mean Christians should become hypocrites or be apathetic or ascetic. They may rejoice or weep with others. But neither laughter nor tears are the final word. They must not let themselves get lost in either. Christians buy and use the world (through commerce and social relations), but they should not be absorbed in these. They must live in the service of the Lord and not become entangled with the world's affairs (read 2 Tim. 2:3-4). The present form of the world is passing away, and the scenes are shifting. Since the child of God may face a new scene tomorrow, he or she should not become entangled with the affairs of this life.

In verses 36-38, the apostle dealt with another issue related to marriage: should engaged couples follow through with their planned marriage? Biblical scholars differ as to whether verse 36 is a reference to a father with a virgin daughter[8] or a man to whom a virgin is betrothed. Verses 37 and 38 clearly refer to the latter:

---

[8] This interpretation suggests that the father does not commit sin by allowing his daughter who is of marriageable age to marry. There are two basic problems with this view: (1) *huperakmos* (King James Version, "past the flower of age") does not normally mean "at the age of marriage." The normal meaning is "strong passions," but can mean "past one's prime, past marriageable age." (2) The word *virgin* does not mean "daughter." A father would not usually think of his marriageable daughter as his virgin. Another interpretation is that the reference is to "spiritual marriage"—a man and woman living together with no physical relations at all. As far as we know, spiritual marriages were not practiced as early as the first century. There were spiritual marriages in the Church perhaps as early as the second century, but we have no record of them as early as Paul's time.

But the man who has settled the matter in his own mind, who is under no compulsion but has control over his own will, and who has made up his mind not to marry the virgin—this man also does the right thing. So then, he who marries the virgin does right, but he who does not marry her does even better (NIV).

Apparently, the man and woman were engaged. Among the Corinthian believers were ascetics who taught that sex and marriage were not for truly spiritual people. Likely, they insisted that the couple should remain as they were. Due to the influence of the ascetics, the man might have felt that it would be uncomely (*aschemonein* or "to behave in an unseemly, dishonorable way") to consummate their marriage. It may seem strange to speak of the man's fiancée as his virgin, but the woman in question was a virgin.

Paul's advice was that if the man had strong passions, he should marry. A man who married his sweetheart did well, but the one who did not marry her did even better. So the Corinthian inquiry was, "Will it not be better for an engaged couple to refrain from going on to marriage?" Indeed, in view of the difficult circumstances and troubled times, it would have been better; but if they married, they had not sinned. They had done well.

CONCLUSION

The divine order encompasses the home as well as the Church. Both have been appointed by God to share in the responsibilities of Christian discipleship, nurture, witnessing, and service. The home is as strong as the Church helps it to be, and the Church as strong as the home. The Church and the home stand together.

Crucial to the strength of the home is the marriage relationship, in which husbands and wives maintain fidelity. God's order for sex and marriage was not entirely manifested among the Corinthian believers. A number of them had been careless about the marriage bond. Some had not appreciated it as they ought; others did not deem it necessary to limit the most intimate human relationship to it. Many of the tragedies of divorce today have their roots in the attitudes and practices regarding sex found at ancient Corinth.

The Biblical understanding of sex is not that it is the whole of a marital relationship, but that it is only one dimension of a happy marriage. Therefore, Paul did not advocate the suppression of sex in married love as some did at Corinth; nor did he exaggerate it as today's sexually saturated society does when it implies that the full meaning of married love is reached in sex. Either the suppression or the exaltation of sex is contrary to Paul's inspired teaching. Today sex is not only elevated but almost deified. It is not surprising that incidents of premarital and extramarital sexual intercourse are increasing. It is time for the Church, as Paul did, to speak clearly on the question of sexual morality. He spoke with candor on the subject. The Church needs to do likewise.

Briefly, to summarize Paul's view of sex and marriage:

(1) The proper place for sexual expression is marriage. In the context of the love and loyalty of a monogamous home, man's sexual life finds its true good and fulfillment. One purpose of sexual relations is the continuance of the race, but another is the mutual satisfaction of husband and wife. The husband gives his body for the pleasure of his wife, and vice versa (vv. 3-4). Upbuilding and mutuality, basic to Paul's understanding of human relations, should characterize the love of man and wife. Mutual rights and responsibilities begin in the family where husband and wife have mutual rights and responsibilities and share in all dimensions of life.

(2) Marriage is a lifetime relationship. God has consecrated the marriage relationship as indissoluble. Indeed, it is serious business. When both husband and wife are Christians, they are bound by the teaching of Christ. Only death can legitimately release one from the other. If problems develop that make

69

separation the only solution, Paul advised the two to remain single or to restore their marriage. If circumstances make it necessary to tolerate divorce, it is still against God's demand.

The situation becomes more complicated when only one of the marriage partners is a Christian. That a believer lives with an unbeliever provides no ground for the believer to break up the marriage. The dissolving of the relationship should be the last resort. As long as the two live together, the unbeliever is influenced by the believer. The children who grow up in such a home come under the sanctifying influence of the Holy Spirit.

Many delicate problems faced the Corinthians. The truths that Paul shared with them under the guidance of the Holy Spirit can do much to stabilize the family life in our society. If Christians will seek the guidance of God's Spirit and strive no to deviate from the divine order for sex and marriage, much can be done to maintain the Christian home in this day.

CHAPTER 5

THE USE AND ABUSE OF CHRISTIAN FREEDOM
(8:1—11:1)

A notable feature of a Christian congregation is fellowship created by the Holy Spirit. It is a fellowship of holy ones, but the Corinthian congregation was anything but "holy" in terms of life and conduct. Schism marred their fellowship.

At least in part, the divisions in this church were due to differences of opinion about eating meat used in pagan worship. Again, the Corinthians had asked Paul questions. The main query behind 1 Corinthians 8–10 must have been something like this: "How do we reconcile the dispute among us overeating meat offered in idol worship?"

This was a first-century problem; it poses no problem for us today. However, it does now, as it did then, raise an important and much larger issue—the meaning of Christian freedom. Every child of God is faced with the problem of individual freedom and responsibility (or what a Christian can and cannot do).

The issue at Corinth was amoral; that is, the eating of meat was, in itself, neither good nor bad. To eat or to abstain did not necessarily make one a better Christian. It was not moral as doing good to others nor immoral as stealing. In itself, eating meat added nothing nor took anything from the Christian's spiritually.

There were certain Corinthians who understood that it was harmless to eat meat offered as a sacrifice to idols; others took an opposing view. That contributed to a spirit of divisiveness. Whether such grew out of Christians rallying around human personalities (chs. 1–4) or out of conflict over what was right and wrong (chs. 8–10), it was and still is a clear departure from the order prescribed by God for the Church.

Unity of life, as well as holiness and purity, was to be a mark of Christians in the local congregation. The divine order called for the Christians to moderate their individual freedom for the spiritual welfare of others and the upbuilding of the church. This entire section of 1 Corinthians breathes the true spirit of Christian ethics.

THE RELATIONSHIP BETWEEN STRONG AND WEAK CHRISTIANS

The situation at Corinth must have been similar to what Paul found in Athens (Acts 17:16-23). Idols also were prevalent in Corinth. A prominent element of pagan worship in the city was offering animal sacrifices to idols. Portions of the animal sacrifices were disposed of by priests as they saw fit. Much of this meat turned up in the markets for sale. The butchers went down where the sacrifices were offered and bought the meat so they could offer some specials.

As sinners, the Corinthians had patronized the markets and restaurants; but when they became Christians, they questioned, "Should we continue to do this?" Was the meat any different after it had been used in pagan worship?

Some among the Corinthian believers maintained there was no difference and that no harm came from eating meat offered to idols. Those who saw nothing wrong with eating such meat were not designated by Paul as "strong," but an inference can be made from Paul's calling the opposing group "weak" (1 Cor. 8:10-11).

The weak were finicky about eating this meat and worried that the practice might be wrong. They were weak not in their willpower, or in their devotion to God, but in their grasp of the truth and in their knowledge. Paul agreed with those who thought it was right to eat such meat, but he challenged them to exercise their Christian freedom responsibly. Otherwise, they would abuse their freedom and destroy the weaker brothers' faith.

Christians Must Be Guided by Brotherly Love (vv. 1-7). The apostle appealed to the knowledge of the Corinthians. Many of them knew idols were nothing and the so-called gods of the pagans were not gods. Their temptation was to see the eating of sacrificial meat as a sure sign of Christian liberty. They displayed their freedom in the face of other Christians who felt that eating the meat was wrong. There was no doubt that they were enlightened, but their knowledge led them to self-conceit and impatience with those less advanced in understanding.

Superior insight was good, but separated from love it could be dangerous. Mere knowledge tended to "puff up." It was well for them to remember that no man really knew anything as he ought because all things have their explanation in God. At best, human knowledge was limited and imperfect, but for some of the Corinthians it was the ultimate.

Knowledge did have its place in the Christian experience. It revealed that there was but one God; so idols were nothing and the Gentile gods were but figments of men's imagination. Not every Corinthian Christian knew that. Some had, in their recent past, worshiped idols and took them to be real.

Paul did not wish to sell knowledge short, but just to know something about God meant little. Love was the key. Paul reminded his readers that "if any man love God, the same is known of him" (v. 3). A Christian's fellowship with God was based on love. His love for others grew out of his grateful love to God. True

Christian freedom was rooted in a firm grasp of one's faith, but such knowledge operated in love and held the truth in humility.

Regardless of how reliable, knowledge by itself was a poor basis for Christian conduct. If what one did was determined by knowledge alone, he would ask, "Is this right or wrong? Is this permitted or forbidden?" If he was guided by love, he would ask, "Is this helpful or hurtful to someone else?" Knowledge alone made individuals conceited, but love edified others and strengthened the church.

Christian Freedom Must Be Restricted by Brotherly Love (vv. 8-13). Joining the church did not settle all of the Corinthian problems. Each brought from his earlier experiences to the Christian fellowship various attitudes and beliefs, which helped make him what he was. Some of these were not in harmony with the attitudes and beliefs of other Christians. So there were differences of opinion among the Corinthians as to what was right or wrong, especially in the area of the amoral. The weak Corinthians, with an overscrupulous conscience, thought eating sacrificial food made concessions to idols, while the strong had no such scruples.

Paul spoke to both the strong and the weak. Food did not commend anyone to God; it did nothing to improve a Christian's relationship with God. The refusal to eat did not detract from fellowship with God. No man was saved because he was an advanced Christian with superior knowledge or condemned because he followed the scruples of a "weak conscience." No man lost anything by eating nor gained anything by abstaining. Neither the refusal nor the consent to eat made any difference with God.

However, using their freedom to eat sacrificial food, the strong Christians encouraged the weak to follow suit. They ate with clear conscience. By ignoring the effect of their actions on others, they sinned not only against the weak brethren but also against Christ. Although their conscience gave them a green light, that did not mean God had given them a green light. Love, not conscience or knowledge, was the true guide.

Love should have been allowed to settle disputes over matters that were neither right nor wrong in themselves. What was safe for one person might have been unsafe for another. For this reason, what a Christian did was to be determined not by knowledge but by love. Knowledge alone was not enough. Through knowledge, the strong caused the weak brother, for whom Christ died, to stumble. Knowledge did indicate to the strong that they had the right to eat meat, but no man had the liberty to exercise his right if it hurt another.

A Christian had no rights if his rights hindered another. The rule was "if what I eat causes my brother or sister to fall into sin, I will never eat meat again" (v. 13 NIV). Rather than hinder or hurt a weak conscience, Paul preferred never to taste meat again. Christian love, therefore, made it impossible for a believer to exercise his liberties carelessly and to do as he pleased without regard for others. Guided by love, a Christian was aware that he was his brother's keeper and was ready at all times to deny himself for the spiritual benefit of others.

PAUL'S USE OF CHRISTIAN FREEDOM

The apostle freely surrendered his "rights" for the sake of others. Indeed, he was an example of disciplined freedom. As it will become clear from Paul's life, this kind of freedom is responsible and curbs the desire to do absolutely as one pleases.

He Had the Rights (9:1-11). If he had wished, Paul could have lived off the Gospel. But under the circumstances he had foregone his rights:

(1) *To support from the church.* He was free to live as the other

apostles. On the road to Damascus he had seen the Lord, which was essential to qualify him to be an apostle. The Corinthian Church itself was proof of his apostleship. So he had the right to be given food and drink for his work.

(2) *To take a wife with him.* The other apostles had taken their wives with them on trips. The church, too, was obligated to support Paul and his wife, if he had had one.

(3) *To be free from manual labor.* He and Barnabas had worked with their own hands to earn their living. They had the right to eat and drink at the cost of the church. A soldier did not go to war at his own expense; his food, clothing, and weapon were provided by the army. Why should a soldier of Christ have to provide for himself? A man who planted a vineyard was allowed to eat the grapes; he benefited from what he planted. Paul had planted churches. Why should he not benefit from his labor? A shepherd who fed the sheep used the milk from the flock. Why should not those who fed God's flock?

There were everyday examples, but Scripture itself taught the same principle. The law of Moses prohibited the muzzling of an ox while it was treading out the grain (Deut. 25:4). Unthreshed grain was placed on the threshing floor, and an ox was driven over the grain to shake the ripe grain loose from the stalks. Unmuzzled, the ox could eat the grain. God enjoined the practice of not muzzling the ox for the purpose of teaching us something about His kindness.

If consideration was to be shown to a beast of burden, how much more should kindness be shown to every worker! God's kindness extended to everyone who labored, even the ox that threshed the grain. As workers in God's field, Christian ministers had the right to partake of the fruits of their labor. The man who plowed and the man who reaped had hope of getting a share of the crop.

He Waived All These Rights (1 Cor. 9:12-18). The Corinthians knew Paul and his coworkers had sown spiritual seed in Corinth and that they had the right to reap a temporal harvest. Furthermore, the Corinthians knew that even the priests of the idol temples received a share of the worshipers' sacrifices and got their living from the temple resources. "In the same way, the Lord has commanded that those who preach the gospel should receive their living from the gospel" (v. 14 *NIV*). So, as all ministers of the Gospel, Paul and his helpers had the right to receive recompense for their work. It was and still is not too much to expect the church to support its ministers. For spiritual service, a minister can expect a material return. The laborer is worthy of his hire (Luke 10:7; 1 Tim. 5:18).

But Paul had not exercised his rights. He could have eaten at the expense of the church (1 Cor. 9:4); he could have married (v. 5); he could have received a salary for his ministry (vv. 6-7). Rather, Paul had foregone these and had willingly lived by the principle of love laid down in chapter 8.

While making it clear that ministers had the right to receive salaries, Paul refused any material benefits for his work in Corinth. He did this to protect his influence, lest he be a stumbling block to anyone, and to make it clear that his motives were pure. He deliberately refrained from using his rights, lest people suspect his motives. He refused to take anything so that he could not be accused of using religion as a means of making easy money. He exercised his freedom in the interest of the Gospel and his hearers. To have done otherwise could have put an obstacle in the way of others coming to the Savior.

During his eighteen-month stay at Corinth, Paul supported himself by the craft of tent-making (Acts 18:3; 2 Cor. 12:13, 18). He did not always do this, as we learn from Philippians 4:16-17. But he had no plans to claim a salary from the Corinthians. His desire was to continue to preach the Gospel without charge. Like the prophet Jeremiah, he felt fire within his bones when he was silent (Jer. 20:9). "Woe to me if I do not preach the gospel!" (1 Cor. 9:16 NIV).

The stewardship or trust (*oikonomia*)[1] of the Gospel had been committed to him. He was under orders from the risen Christ to discharge his task, but he did it willingly. Evidence of this was that he became a voluntary servant of others without charge, but he was not without reward. He had the satisfaction of taking the Gospel to the unsaved. While Paul was free to claim a living from the preaching of the Gospel, he did not surrender his freedom by his refusal to take advantage of that right. It was precisely this way that he exercised his freedom.

He Obligated Himself to Serve All People (vv. 19-23). As a Christian, the apostle was free from all people, but he made himself a servant to all so he might win as many as possible to Christ. He became all things to all men—not that he had no convictions, not that he was two-faced (saying one thing to one and something just the opposite to another), nor that he compromised the truth of God's Word. But he was able to be at home with everyone.

He knew how to accommodate his notions and manners to those of others, so far as his duty to God would permit. He was ready to make concessions to people, as long as he could act without violation to Christian precepts. To all men he became all things.[2]

To the Jew he became a Jew, abstaining from forbidden meats and giving careful attention to the observance of the Law. To the Gentile he lived as a Gentile, nor forcing on anyone circumcision and other nonessentials of Judaism. To the weaker brothers, the

---

[1] In 1 Cor. 10:17 in the Authorized Version (King James), *oikonomia* is rendered *dispensation*, but it is better translated "stewardship" or "trust."

[2] Acts 13 and 14 provide excellent examples of this principle.

ones who had religious scruples such as eating meat that had been offered to idols, he became like one of them.

All of this was done that he might share the benefits of the Gospel with as many as possible. He adjusted his lifestyle and approach so he should not offend those whom he sought to win. His constant concern for others overruled what might have been a legitimate use of Christian freedom. So he became all things to all men, adapting himself to their customs and needs, for no other purpose than to share with them the blessings of the Gospel.

He Practiced Self-Discipline (vv. 24-27). No one knew better than Paul the importance of moral and spiritual discipline in the Christian life. Corinth was the seat for the Isthmian games. These, which were second only to the Olympic Games, provided Paul with a ready illustration.

The athletes who participated underwent demanding self-discipline and rigorous training. They were put on a strict diet, and were required to abstain from wine and to train for ten months under the watchful eye of the judges. All of the contestants submitted to strict discipline with the hope of winning the coveted crown that would be awarded only to the winner. The crown meant much more to them that it was worth. It was just a wreath, which in a few days would wither, but the accolades and acclaim bestowed on the one who won the race made it highly coveted.

The athletes subjected themselves to the rigid self-discipline to win a fading wreath. Likewise, Paul knew Christians were to practice self-denial that they might win an unfading wreath, a crown of life. That could not be done without the self-discipline that marked the training of the competitors in the Greek games.

As a Christian, Paul lived a disciplined life. He knew where he was going. He pursued not comfort, money, respect, or position, but the kingdom of God. He ran with determination and was unlike a boxer who beats the air and wastes his punches. His blows hit their mark, his opponent being himself. "I keep under my body[3] [more literally, 'I beat myself black and blue'], and bring it into subjection: lest . . . when I have preached to others, I myself should be a castaway" (v. 27). He wanted nothing to happen that would disqualify him from receiving the ultimate prize of salvation.

As Paul indicated from his own experience, discipline in the life of the Christian is vital. Indulgence and uncontrolled desires hinder the Christian work and jeopardize one's relationship with Jesus Christ. The Christian must constantly be on guard to avoid the ways of the ungodly.

In summary then, true freedom for Paul was the fruit of discipline. While he did speak of the negative side of Christian freedom as deliverance "from the law of sin and death" (Rom. 8:2), his positive note was the main one: freedom "for" rather than freedom "from." "It is for freedom that Christ has set us free. Stand firm, then, and do not let yourselves be burdened again by a yoke of slavery" (Gal. 5:1 *NIV*).

Christian freedom was not undisciplined license, but power for the fulfillment of the demands of Christ. The Savior empowered Paul from within to fulfill what he ought to be and do. It was freedom "for," as is clearly borne out by the three reasons he gave in 1 Corinthians 9 for limiting the exercise of his personal liberties: (1) for the sake of the Gospel (vv. 15-18, 23), (2) for the sake of souls (vv. 19-22), and (3) for the sake of self-mastery (vv. 24-27).

THE USE OF FREEDOM WITH A SENSE OF OBLIGATION

A Warning Against Overconfidence (10:1-13). Above, we saw a positive example of what Christian freedom meant, but Paul

---

[3] *Body (sōma)* refers to Paul's total personality rather than to just his physical constitution. He exercised complete control of himself.

went on to appeal to examples from Hebrew history.[4] These concerned the people of God who started well and enjoyed spiritual advantages. But, because of self-indulgence and a lack of self-discipline, they were chastened severely by God.

The Corinthians were reminded by Paul that spiritual benefits were not a guarantee against the chastening hand of God. No people were more blessed than the Israelites whom God led from Egyptian bondage unto liberty. The fact that Paul placed emphasis on "all," repeating it five times, served to point out the high privileges Israel once enjoyed.

They were all under the pillar of cloud by day and the pillar of fire by night, which became a guide to them on their journey (v. 1; Ex. 13:21-22). All were brought miraculously through the Red Sea (v. 1; Ex. 14:21-22). They all were baptized into Moses in the cloud and in the sea (v. 2); that is, the experiences related to the cloud and the sea brought them into a close personal relationship with Moses and to an acceptance of his leadership. Thus, they pledged to follow him. All ate the same spiritual bread, the manna God provided in the wilderness (v. 3; Ex. 16:35). All drank the same spiritual drink which was from a spiritual rock, which was Christ (v. 4; Ex. 17:1-7).[5]

In spite of all these wonderful blessings, many of the Israelites displeased God. Only two pleased Him—Joshua and Caleb (Num. 32:11-12). The rest of the people "were overthrown in the wilderness" (v. 5), and their dead bodies were scattered over the desert.

---

[4] The account of Israel's deliverance from Egypt and the wandering in the wilderness as recorded in Exodus and Numbers is the background in verses 1-13.

[5] There was a rabbinic legend that suggested that the rock at Rephidim accompanied Israel. Paul did not rely on the legend. The language he employed was a vivid way of saying that Christ was with Israel and that Israel spiritually drank of Christ. The "spiritual Rock," Christ himself, followed His people to supply their needs.

The failures of Israel, Paul reminded the self-satisfied Corinthians, were warnings to them. He called on his readers to learn from history, which made it clear that the Israelites were severely chastened for disobeying God.

(1) *Israel committed idolatry.* While Moses was on Mount Sinai, the people prevailed upon Aaron to make a golden calf (Ex. 32:1-5). They sat down to an idol feast. From this feast they arose to indulge in idolatrous revelry (vv. 6, 19). They were singing and dancing around the golden calf when Moses descended bearing the tables of the Law.

(1) *Israel committed fornication.* After having committed sexual immorality with the Midianites and Moabites, twenty-three thousand perished on a single day (Num. 25:1-9).

(1) *Israel tried the patience of the Lord* (cf. Deut. 6:16; Matt. 4:7). Presuming on God's goodness, a number of the people complained and murmured against Him, and fell victims to snakes (Num. 21:1-9). Too, some murmured and grumbled against Moses and Aaron and were struck down by the angel of death (16:41-50).

These things had happened in the ages past, but they were recorded in Scripture as warnings to those "upon whom the ends of the world [*ta tete ton aionon,* 'the ends of the ages'] are come" (1 Cor. 10:11). This phrase indicated the Corinthians as well as all Christians, since the death and resurrection of Christ, were living at a point in time where "the present age" and "the coming age" overlap.[6] The future Kingdom had been brought in measure within the experience of the Christian by Christ.

Living in such a favored position, no believer should have been too confident that he could stand (v. 12). A number of the

---

[6] See Arrington, *op. cit.,* pp. 129-32, 145-50, for an exposition of the Church as an eschatological community which consists of men who live in the Messianic times "upon whom the ages have come."

Corinthians saw no danger of their becoming involved in idolatry and no risk in being attracted to the idol feasts in Corinth. Some were seeing how close they could get to sin. No man should have let down his guard. Paul reminded the Corinthians that the Israelites who enjoyed so many divine blessings did, and their skeletons were scattered over the wilderness.

To counter their smug self-confidence, Paul warned the Corinthians that he who thought he stood should beware "lest he fall" as did those Israelites of old. Temptation was certain to come, but those who relied on God would find a way of escape. Not that temptation would be removed, but God would not allow them to be tempted beyond resistance without providing a route of escape (v. 13). In temptation, the sufficiency of God's grace is ministered not to the self-reliant but to the "God-reliant."[7] The Christian who trusts in God day by day can win victory amid the daily temptations of the world and Satan.

A Warning Against Idolatry (vv. 14-22). There is a return to the difficulty with which this section of the epistle opens; namely, eating meat that had been consecrated to pagan worship. Apparently, the Corinthians who did not hesitate to eat what had been sacrificed to the idols thought also that they could participate in the pagan feasts and worship. While the use of such meat fell in the realm of moral indifference, it took on a different color when Christians participated in meals at an idol temple.

Idolatry was definitely wrong. While the pagan gods did not actually exist, demons did. Demonic powers stood behind pagan feasts and ceremonies, however meaningless they might have seemed to the Corinthians. Meat offered to idols was really offered to demons. A Christian who participated in such worship became a partner with the demons.

At Corinth some of the believers had attended heathen feasts.

---

[7] Julian C. McPheeters, *The Epistles to the Corinthians*, p. 46.

They took their liberty to a sinful extreme. Paul pointed out their inconsistency: "Ye cannot drink the cup of the Lord, and the cup of devils: ye cannot be partakers of the Lord's table, and of the table of devils" (v. 21). This alluded to the ordinance of the Lord's Supper. In the Supper the cup was the "communion of the blood of Christ" (v. 16).

Here the word for *communion (koinonia)* is rendered *fellowship* in 1 Corinthians 1:9, and it basically means "partaking" or "sharing." The bread was "communion" with the body of Christ, which referred to the Church (the fellowship of believers). The Corinthians proclaimed in their celebration of the Supper that they had fellowship with "the blood of Christ"; that is, they shared in the saving benefits secured by His death.

There was yet another dimension of fellowship in it— communion among believers, "the body of Christ" (v. 16). The common sharing in Christ's redeeming blood was expressed concretely in their fellowship with one another.

While each was an individual, they had become in Christ members of one body, the body of Christ. Partaking of the one bread in the Supper, the Corinthians became one. The one loaf of which they ate and by which they were united symbolized the true bread of life (John 6).

Still another example of this was historic Israel (literally in v. 18, "Israel [according to] the flesh"). The Israelites all ate of the sacrifices from the same altar. Thus, they were united by the altar and were put under the influence of Jehovah. Likewise, in celebrating the Lord's Supper, the Corinthians were united with one another and enjoyed communion with the Lord.

The same applied to feasting with idolaters. Some of the Corinthians came to the Lord's table after having participated in pagan feasts. The pagans offered their sacrifices to demons. No one who belonged to the fellowship of Christ's body (the Church) should have exposed himself to demon worship. So Paul urged the Corinthians to "flee from idolatry" (v. 14). By participating in such, they became partners with demons.

They could not share in the cup of the Lord and the cup or food of demons. They could not be guests of the Lord and, at the same time, guests of demons. They could not share in the worship of God one day and then share in the worship of demons the next. There was no communion between the Lord and the devil. It was unthinkable that one could worship Christ and have fellowship with Him and, at the same time, have communion with demons. Paul warned his readers that the attempt to worship God and demons would provoke divine jealously.[8]

Some of the Corinthians were seeing how close to sin they could get, but as Saint Augustine so aptly said, "He that will go as near the ditch as he can, will at some time or other fall in; so he that will take all liberty that possibly he may lawfully, cannot but fall into many unlawful things."[9]

The Use of Christian Freedom for the Sake of Others (10:23–11:1). Paul showed that the danger of idol worship was more real and subtle than what the Corinthians thought. Idol worship was demonic. So he went on to pick up the topical discussion of chapter 8—meat offered to idols when served in a home. His concern was not so much with the strong as with their responsibility toward those who thought it was improper to eat sacrificial meat.

The apostle began by repeating a slogan: "All things are lawful" (v. 23), which had been used by the Corinthians in defense of eating meat offered to idols and of indulging in other questionable

---

[8] The implication was that the Corinthians were not to engage at all in idolatry. Paul reminded the Thessalonians that they "[had] turned to God from idols to serve the living and true God" (1 Thess. 1:9). The point is clear that they were to have nothing to do with pagan worship and were to be content with serving the only true God.

[9] Cited in *Gray and Adams Bible Commentary*, p. 140.

pursuits. Certainly what was not sinful in itself was lawful, but all that was lawful was "not expedient"; that is, helpful, profitable, and wise to do. All things lawful did not "edify"; that is, build up individual believers in the faith. The apostle insisted that Christian liberty must be limited for the sake of others. "No one should seek their own good, but the good of others" (v. 24 *NIV*).

Regarding the purchase of meat in the market and any scruples about eating it, Paul's advice was twofold:

(1) Anything sold in the meat market[10] could be eaten. Meat in any of the shops could have been offered as a sacrifice to a god. Asking no questions, the believer could eat it. It was possible to be too fussy and to create needless problems. In the final analysis, all things belonged to the Lord (v. 26).

(2) If an unsaved friend invited a believer to dinner, the believer was to eat the meat set before him and ask no questions. However, if a brother told him that it had been offered to an idol, the believer was not to eat it. The reason was that the brother who told him associated it with pagan worship. To abstain out of the respect for the brother's conscience was Paul's advice.

Apparently the following questions had been raised by the Corinthians: "For why is my freedom being judged by another's conscience? If I take part in the meal with thankfulness, why am I denounced because of something I thank God for? (vv. 29-30 *NIV*). Paul's answer was, "So whether you eat or drink or whatever you do, do it all for the glory of God. Do not cause anyone to stumble,[11] whether Jews, Greeks or the church of God" (vv. 31-32).

The immediate reference was eating sacrificial meat, yet the principle has a much broader application in the Christian life.

---

[10] In verse 24, *shambles* (*makellon*) referred to the place where meat and other articles of food were sold; it was a meat market.

[11] The instruction "give none offence" means not to put a stumbling block in the way of any person, whether Jew, Gentile, or Christian.

All that a Christian does should have one aim—to glorify God. Christian liberty must be used to help rather than to hinder others. As Christians, the Corinthian believers were duty bound to all men—not only to fellow believers, but also to Jews and Gentiles still unsaved. In fulfilling this obligation, they were to bring glory to God and salvation to souls. They were to guide the course of their conduct with their eyes and thought on others, so as to avoid laying a stumbling block before anyone. Paul said, "Be ye followers of me, even as I also am of Christ" (11:1). He did not seek his own advantage or pleasure; neither should they. His aim was the glory of God, the salvation of souls, and the edification of the Church.

CONCLUSION
To maintain proper order in the church, Christians must subordinate their rights and privileges to their obligations and duties. When Christians become preoccupied with personal rights, they bring division into the church and violate the Christian law of love. Liberty in Christ is not to be used selfishly but benevolently.

From our study in 1 Corinthians 8:1–11:1, a number of enduring truths have emerged:

(1) *Whatever we do must be to God's glory and for the spiritual good of others.* This principle is far wider that the issue at Corinth; for if we live for the glory of God as Paul did, we shall be ready to limit our freedom of action and to refrain from things lawful to us. Therefore, we dare not decide any question merely as to whether it is right or wrong for us. This leaves out the judgment and conscience of others altogether and is too selfish.

Sadly, we have not escaped the scourge of selfishness, especially when a church does everything possible to entice members away from another church of the same denomination and Christians live by the code: "Every man for himself." Such is utterly incompatible with true Christianity.

Our great concern should be this, that we honor God in all things and voluntarily forego certain rights for the edification of others. This does not involve denying our individuality nor allowing people to trample over us. Paul defended the Gospel and his ministry against his opponents while living for the glory of God and building believers up in the faith.

(2) *Eating one kind of food and abstaining from another does not commend us to God.* Our personal relation to Christ is not a matter of diet, but faith in His life and death. There is no special Christian grace in eating nor in abstaining. "But food does not bring us near to God; we are no worse if we do not eat, and no better if we do" (1 Cor. 8:8 *NIV*). If we decide not to eat a food, we should not impose this restriction on others.

(3) *We are responsible for the influence of our conduct on weaker Christians.* Not that their weakness is the yardstick or the standard for the Church. Paul made no attempt to reduce the strong to the level of the weak. The weak ought to grow strong. The way to make them strong is to avoid laying a cause of stumbling in their way and to show them loving consideration. (Read Rom. 14:13; 15:1.) It takes some longer to grow strong than others and to come to a full grasp of the truth. Forbearance and love enable them to gain the strength and understanding of the Gospel they need. No child of God needs to remain immature and to be preoccupied with things incidental to his or her faith.

(4) *Not superior knowledge but love is the true guide for Christian conduct.* Knowledge is desirable and needed, but without love it can puff up and lead us to the sad error of supposing that abstinence is always a matter of weakness and to its companion error that participation at will in anything and everything is a sign of strength. To know what is not unclean and sinful in itself is to have strong mature insight into Christian conduct, but to be ready to deny self for the benefit of others is to be strong in love.

(5) *Some things are always worldly, carnal, and morally wrong, but others are neither essentially good or bad.* If an activity is not wrong in itself, should we participate? Should we break with certain associations, cease to be entertained by worldly friends, to go here or there? Remember: what we do with safety may be unsafe for another and may cause him to stumble. The final test for us is not whether we can or cannot do a certain thing, but whether our doing it will help or hinder others.

CHAPTER 6

THE BREAKING OF RELIGIOUS CUSTOMS
(11:2-34)

Carnality was far-reaching at Corinth, affecting not only the lives of believers but also the public worship. There were three major problems that gave rise to disorder in the church gatherings. The first was women refusing to wear their veils, the second was abuses at the Lord's Supper, and the third was the improper use of spiritual gifts.

The first two of these are discussed in chapter 11. A much larger section (chs. 12–14) is devoted to the discussion of the gifts of the Spirit. These practices—as well as gross immorality (6:12-20) and participating in feasts at idol temples (8:10; 10:21)—were instances of the reckless use of a newfound freedom. As already noted, one of the Corinthians' slogans was, "All things are lawful unto me" (6:12; 10:23).

We read in chapter 11 that the same spirit sought to flaunt the social custom of women veiling their heads and to convert the Lord's Supper to divisive cliques and an occasion for gluttony. A custom in the early church was the *agape* or love feast—a social gathering in which the rich and poor pooled their food to make a common feast. Abuses in the feast were carried over into the celebration of the Supper.

In his reply to questions about order in worship, Paul dealt first with the place of the Christian woman within the church and second with the observance of the Lord's Supper. The Corinthians had no right to transgress the prevailing religious customs, but regretfully that was exactly what they were doing. To curb this, Paul urged the women to wear their veils in public worship and the entire church to observe the Lord's Supper in a bond of mutual affection and in a manner worthy of its character.

PROPER ORDER OF RELATIONSHIPS

The general feeling in ancient Greece was that women were inferior to men and, at best, second-class citizens. Unlike most of the Greek mystery religions, Christianity did not exclude women from membership. It was great news to women when Paul announced that Jesus Christ died for them and there was neither male nor female in Christ (Gal. 3:28). When women repented of their sins and accepted Christ as their Savior, they were received into the church at par with the men.

The newfound freedom was relished by the Corinthian women. But they carried this liberty in Christ to unfortunate extremes, failing to distinguish between their spiritual freedom and their social status. As a result, they probably reasoned that if they and their husbands were spiritual equals in Christ, there was no need for them to wear any longer the sign of submission to their husbands at the activities of the church. So they were laying aside the veil, which women wore at the time to cover their hair and foreheads.

The veil was more than just an item of dress. It was a badge of a woman's dignity and chastity as well as submission to her husband. A lady did not appear unveiled outside of her home. Otherwise, she was no lady. At Corinth, the Christian women were leaving the wrong impression by discarding the customs of modesty of that day. To the outsiders, they were women of easy virtue and perhaps members of the Aphrodite cult (sacred prostitutes). The good name of the church was suffering.

To deal with the quest of the women for equality, Paul reminded them of the divine order of relationships: God is the head of Christ; Christ, of man; and man, of woman. This chain suggests originating and subordinating relationships.

In the Old Testament, the word *head* (*rosh*) refers to rank. For example, it is used of the ruler of the community (Judg. 10:18); of God—"Thou art exalted as head above all" (1 Chron. 29:11); and of the Messiah—the stone has become the head of the corner (Ps. 118:22).

In Greek thought, *head* (*kephale*) often signifies the outstanding part or origin of something. The latter is strongly suggested by verse 8: "Man was not made from woman but woman from man."[1] Adam was first created, and then to provide him with a helper, God took Eve from Adam's side (cf. Gen. 2:18-23).

Paul's concern was seniority, not superiority. He did not teach that man was the lord of woman but that man was the source of her being. That God is the head of Christ can be understood in a similar way. Christ was neither created nor was He inferior to the Father in His spiritual essence. His existence is in God as the woman's is in man. He is fully and completely God as woman is fully and completely human. Woman is given in the existence of man; Christ is given in the existence of God.

Furthermore, Christ is the head of every man. It is well to note that Christ is the source of the being of all people, not just Christians. He is the ground and origin of humanity. He was the agent of creation as well as redemption. "For by him were all things created" (Col. 1:16). "One Lord Jesus Christ, by whom are all things" (1 Cor. 8:6).

---

[1] Author's translation

Although Christ was equal to the Father, the eternal Son voluntarily became obedient and submissive to Him. To accomplish the mission to redeem humankind from sin, Christ brought Himself under the will of the heavenly Father. So, in the society of the Godhead is an order for the execution of the divine will.

The same principle applies to the husband-wife relationship. As there are rank and order in the divine society, so there are also rank and order within the human family. This is suggested by the fact that Eve was made from Adam and for him, and that woman is the glory of man (11:7). This applies directly to the marriage relationship; and, too, Paul took for granted a degree of subordination of the woman to her husband.[2] Man and woman in Christ are spiritually equal; but the divine order of the sexes, which included the family headship of man, was not to be violated in the church.

The order did not involve injustice, humiliation, harshness, or dominance, but rather a distinction in roles and responsibilities. The husband was to be the head of his home and the priest of his family. So Paul did not respond favorably to the view that in Christ all distinctions between male and female had disappeared. He would have nothing of the blurring of the differences ordained by God between men and women.

PROPER DRESS OF MEN AND WOMEN IN WORSHIP

Paul drew attention to some of the implications that the order of authority has for public worship. The apostle laid a heavy burden on both men and women to preserve order within the church.

Men Were to Worship Uncovered (vv. 4, 7). When men took

---

[2] Spittler, *op. cit.*, p. 55, clearly distinguishes subordination from inferiority. "*Subordination* is a matter of rank, of organization. Inferiority is a matter of nature, of quality. What is subordinate is not necessarily inferior. *Inferiority* suggests an inner essential difference. But Paul is not saying women are inferior: he is saying they should be subordinate. And from here he goes on to urge continued use of the veil, the symbol of subordination."

part in worship, they were to be bareheaded.[3] A man covering his head disgraced it (v. 4). It is hard to decide exactly what Paul had in mind, but there are two interpretations of the phrase "disgraced his head":

(1) *The physical head of man.* If this is correct, *head* here refers to the same as in the expression "having his head covered." The uncovered head, according to this, was a sign that man was "the image and glory of God" (v. 7). It was thought by Paul that God's image, in some sense, resided in man's head. If man veiled his head, he would obscure God's image and glory. So, it would be a disgrace for man to cover his head in worship.

(2) *The head of every man—Christ.* A man with a veil would rob his head of its chief function—reflecting the glory of Christ. By this, Christ would be robbed of the mirror in which His glory was reflected. This is probably what Paul had in view. If so, the uncovered head of man in worship betokened the glory and supremacy of the head of all men.

What provoked Paul's words regarding the conduct of men was that they had taken part in worship with their heads uncovered. They had contributed their fair share to the disorder that prevailed in the Christian community at Corinth. Paul's concern was to restore order in the church. By his corrections of male conduct, he made it clear that the men also were responsible for the restoration of order.

---

[3] This was the reverse of Jewish practice. The Jewish men as well as women have customarily expressed their reverence for God by worshiping with their heads covered. However, it is not certain that this custom prevailed among Jewish men in the first century. It is clear that they did not observe this custom in the Corinthian Church. This might have been due to the fact that men in Greece ordinarily worshiped bareheaded, and Corinth was more Greek than Jewish. It is quite possible that Christian men, as opposed to the Jews, prayed with uncovered heads, following the example of Jesus.

Women Were to Worship Covered (vv. 6-16). At Corinth, women prayed and prophesied in public worship.[4] The apostle did not disapprove, provided they were veiled.[5] The man disgraced his head by wearing a veil; the woman, by not wearing one. Some take *head* here to refer to the husband, but the reference to shorn or shaven hair suggests that the physical head is meant (v. 6).

The apostle put forward his reasons why Christian women at Corinth were to observe the social convention of wearing veils:

(1) *Creation declared the same thing (vv. 7-9).* Woman came from man and was the glory of man. Like man, she was created in the image of God, but she was intended to be man's helper. Then creation itself indicated that "woman is the glory of the man" (v. 7). If she prayed or prophesied with her head uncovered, she reflected the glory of man (her head) rather than the glory of God. In her being, she was the glory of man, but in worship she was to glorify only God.

(2) *The angels present in the congregation would be offended by this departure from the order prescribed by creation (v. 10).* What the reference to angels means here is uncertain; but in view of 1 Cor. 4:9 (where apostles are referred to as "a spectacle unto the

---

[4] Some have understood 1 Cor. 14:33-36 (where women were told to remain silent in the church) to contradict 11:5, 13 (which allowed women to pray and prophesy in public worship, as long as they were veiled.) If there had been a contradiction, it is certain Paul would not have let both passages stand in this epistle. The contributions of Christian women were in order, but in chapter 14, Paul commanded them to be silent for the same reason that he did those who spoke in tongues with no interpretation. Uninterpreted tongues did not edify the church, nor did the talk of some of the women at Corinth. In the interest of peace and order, they were commanded to be silent. Heated arguments gave rise to the command: "God is not the author of confusion, but of peace" (v. 33).

[5] Paul was no culture-bound male chauvinist. Many of his views were contrary to those of his Jewish background. For example, he expected women to take an active role in the worship and ministry of the church and referred to women as his coworkers. See Philippians 4:2-3 (Euodias and Syntyche who "labored with me in the gospel"), 1 Corinthians 16:19 ("Aquila and Priscilla salute you . . . with the church that is in their house"), and Romans 16. He said nothing to distinguish the kind of work the women were doing from that of the men.

world and to angels, and to men") likely the apostle though of angels as guardians of the created order. Any departure from the order set forth in creation—where man is the head of woman— would have offended them. This meant that good angels were present with the Corinthian believers at worship and that it was important what the angels saw in the congregation. Anything not done decently and in order would have offended them. So the women were to wear their veils "because of the angels."

Paul urged that the woman should have power (*exousia*, "authority") on her head, which, to say the least, is somewhat surprising. One the basis of what Paul had said, we would expect *veil*, not *authority*. The term *authority* seems to have been another way of speaking of the veil, which was a sign of the woman's authority and dignity—a sign of her womanhood and virtue. An uncovered woman in public was assumed to have low morals. Without the veil the woman was nothing. It was the symbol of her respectability. By discarding her veil, the woman offended the angels present in public worship and brought reproach on Christ and on herself.

(3) *The nature of women called for the same.* Paul appealed to the Corinthians to use their mental power: "Judge for yourselves: Is it proper for a woman to pray to God with her head uncovered?" (v. 13 NIV). God had made man and woman different from each other. An outward sign of the distinction was the quantity of hair He assigned to each. Nature (*physis*) itself taught that it was a dishonor for man to have long hair. On the other hand, a woman's long hair was her glory. Men and women gave glory to God by being what He intended them to be (v. 7); they also honored or showed respect for themselves. For the woman to wear her hair unshorn[6] was a mark of her God-given womanhood and that she

---

[6] According to verse 5, an unveiled head was the same thing as a shaved head. A number of shorn women (*he exuremene*) might have been among Paul's converts at Corinth. There is some evidence from secular writers that shorn hair was a mark of prostitutes. As we have noted there were great hordes who were associated with the temple of Aphrodite in Corinth. Shorn hair among the Jews was a sign of mourning (Jer. 7:29; Mic. 1:16). This does not seem to apply in 1 Corinthians 11.

was fulfilling her purpose in creation. It was not fitting for the woman to cut all of her hair off and obliterate the visible sign that distinguished the sexes.

The woman's hair was part of her endowment by nature; it had been given to her as a form of covering and a visible sign of her femininity. It was her glory—her pride. She was to cover it so that she could present herself in worship in dignity and humility.

(4) *The custom of the churches called for it (v. 16).* Divergence of opinion could not be avoided. If someone remained contentious about women praying and prophesying uncovered, Paul reminded him that the church had not introduced such a custom. The local churches of the first century had their own particular individualities, but they did not differ regarding the social custom under discussion. If there were those who would argue with Paul about the matter, they would be placing themselves in the minority.

PROPER OBSERVANCE OF THE LORD'S SUPPER

The apostle moved on to another point of order in the Corinthian Church, that of conduct at the Lord's Supper. Again he noted there were divisions among the Corinthians, but this time the divisions were between the rich and the poor. The rich feasted; the poor looked on and were hungered (v. 21). Their celebration of the Lord's Supper should have been a profound expression of the unity of the church, but their pride and lack of concern for one another were glaringly evident in the holy meal. As they shared together in the Supper, their unity was to be renewed and strengthened. On the contrary, among the Corinthians the observance of the Supper was an occasion for divisiveness. They carried their quarrels and rivalries over into their fellowship meals (called "love feasts") and into worship.

Divisions at the Love Feast and the Lord's Supper (11:17-22). Prior to the observance of the Lord's Supper, these early Christians had a love feast.[7] It was an ordinary fellowship meal in which the rich who had much food could share with the poor who had little. Therefore, the love feast originated to give Christians who could hardly afford to bring anything an opportunity to get a good meal. But that was not always the result; the love feast at Corinth, for instance, was not a love feast at all. There was no spirit of fellowship, and what went on was shameful. The masters and rich gorged themselves and drank to excess while the servants and poor went hungry. Due to their excess, they were in no condition to participate in one of the most sacred acts of worship, the Lord's Supper.

Paul had heard of the selfish and greedy behavior at the love feasts and at the Lord's table. He partly believed what he had heard and found nothing to praise about such disgraceful conduct. It was better for the people to eat their regular meals at home, if they wanted nothing more than that, rather than to disgrace the church of God (v. 22). Their sin was that they ate as though it were a private meal for individuals or groups. They showed disrespect to the church and insulted the poor who could bring only a little food. They would have done well to remember that God had called into the church not many wise, not many mighty, and not many noble (1 Cor. 1:26).

Sadly, they were destroying the unity and fellowship of the church. After such inconsiderate and carnal behavior, how could they come to the Lord's Supper, which set forth God's redemptive love for all people? Their carnality (selfishness, gluttony, and

---

[7] The love or agape feast was a custom that developed in the early church (cf. Jude 1:12; 2 Peter 2:13). It was never considered an ordinance by the Church, nor is its observance commanded anywhere in Scripture. Because of the excesses associated with the feast at Corinth, Paul advised that it be separated from the Communion and that the Corinthians eat their ordinary meals at home (v. 22). Such advise was due to the Corinthians' disgraceful conduct and provides no basis for condemning fellowship meals at the church where decency is the rule.

drunkenness) denied the meaning of the holy meal and made it a mockery. The Church today needs to be on constant alert against such. How often do modern Christians deny by their conduct and attitudes the very spirit of worship?

The Institution and Significance of the Supper (11:23-25). Seeing to encourage the Corinthians to worship in a proper manner, Paul reminded them that the Supper was received from the Lord. The Holy Communion went back directly to the Lord (Mark 14:22-24). On the night He was betrayed, He took bread and broke it and gave it to His disciples. Likewise, He took the cup and gave it to them to drink. This ordinance came ultimately from the Lord, but Paul either received it from Christians who reported what Christ had done and said,[8] or Christ revealed this truth to him.

The apostle had once delivered to the Corinthians what he had received; but they had forgotten, and he had to repeat it again. Indeed, they had turned the Supper into a frolic and had neglected its real meaning. Aware of that, Paul related the original religious significance of the ceremony.

The bread and cup are signs of the death of Christ; the broken bread signifies His body that was given to death. Our Lord's words "This is my body" (1 Cor. 11:24) should not be interpreted with crude literalism. At that time He was physically present. His body was distinct from the bread. It would be a mistake to assume that He could have held His body in His own hands. Too, the cup is a sign—a sign of His shed blood.

The "new testament," which is better rendered *covenant* (*diatheke*), was sealed with His blood. A covenant is a relationship. At Mount Sinai, God entered into a covenant with Israel, but through Jesus Christ a new relationship has been offered to man.

---

[8] A number of Biblical scholars feel the account of the Supper was passed on to Paul by his predecessors in the Church. The words *received* (*parelabon*) and *delivered* (*paredoka*) are the technical terms for the reception and transmission of religious traditions.

The new covenant cost Christ His life. Christ's blood made that relationship valid.

The Supper looks in two directions: backward to the death of Christ and forward to His second coming. "For as often as ye eat this bread, and drink this cup, ye do shew [*katanggellete*, 'preach' or 'proclaim'] the Lord's death till he come" (v. 26). The Supper has its appointed place in the Church between the two advents of Christ. When believers gather around the table of the Lord, they look backward to the Lord's triumphant death and forward to His final victory when He will come to establish fully the kingdom of God.

Two truths in particular are noteworthy here:

(1) *Christ's death is proclaimed at each observance.* Someone has said that the Holy Supper is the great preacher of the death of Christ. In it, His death for humankind is set before man's eyes. The broken bread and the cup so vividly portray His suffering so as to set the spectacle of the Cross before the eyes of the worshipers. It is an acted-out sermon.

(2) *At the Supper, believers look ahead to the time when Christ will return in glory.* Believers have not yet received the full inheritance that is being kept for them in heaven. Their eyes are fixed on what is expected at the Second Coming. The holy meal tells them of Christ's death until He comes and foreshadows the heavenly banquet, the marriage supper of the Lamb. Understandably the early Christians prayed around the Lord's table, "*Maranatha*"—"Lord, come!" Thus, the Supper not only reminds the Church of a past event, but proclaims the beginning of the time of salvation and anticipates the complete fulfillment at the return of Christ.

Sacredness of the Supper (vv. 26-34). These verses return to the problem with suggestions and explanations. Irregularities at the Lord's table, such as prevailed at Corinth, destroyed the meaning of the holy meal. Anyone guilty was eating and drinking in an unworthy manner. "Unworthily" (v. 27) did not refer to the character of the participants[9] but to their behavior at the Supper. All could approach and celebrate the Holy Communion properly.

By their scandalous conduct, the Corinthians were "guilty of the body and blood of the Lord" (v. 27). Here *body* (*soma*) must refer to the Church, the fellowship of believers (cf. 1 Cor. 12:12-27; Col. 1:24). It is described as the "body of Christ" because there is a close link between Christ and His church and primarily through the Church He continues to accomplish His purpose of saving people.

Paul reminded his readers that individuals who approached this meal in an improper manner were "not discerning the Lord's body" (v. 29); that is, they were not judging the church rightly. The status-conscious Corinthians (perhaps the rich and masters) looked down upon other members of the congregation. From the world's point of view, not many of the early Christians were considered wise or powerful or noble. Divine wisdom, of which a number of Corinthians were devoid, would have issued into a proper discernment of the body of Christ; that is, a spiritual reading of the other members of the Christian fellowship that would have made them aware that their personal, social, cultural, racial, and economic differences were held in the Lord. None of these were foreign to Him.

Paul advised every Corinthian to examine himself to see if he had been doing the things described in verses 18-22. This was good advice. Anyone guilty of such indiscreet conduct had not judged properly what he was destroying—the fellowship of

---

[9] Some Christians have stayed away from the Lord's Supper because they feel unworthy. The warning in 1 Corinthians 11:27 does not denote moral quality of character but an attitude and conduct determined by the Gospel. To approach the Supper "in an unworthy manner" is described in verses 18-22. Christians who are tempted and are having a struggle in living the Christian life especially need to receive the Lord's Supper.

believers—and had shown irreverence to Christ who lived in all of His people. Their lack of reverence in the Supper showed, too, that they did not discern the real significance of Christ's blood; they were guilty of depreciating Christ as the atoning Savior and putting themselves on the side of His enemies.

As a result, the Corinthians could see about them the evidence of the direct judgment of God. There were many cases of sickness at Corinth. Some had even died. All physical afflictions are not due to the punishment of sin, but apparently some are.

Paul offered a word of comfort, telling the Corinthians that the one who judged himself correctly would be spared the judgment of the Lord. So, the final plea was that they be diligent in examining their motives and thoughts and stop their irregularities at Communion so the unity of the church might be demonstrated as they "tarry one for another" (v. 33).

CONCLUSION

One of the most striking features of life in the early church was its sense of fellowship. "They continued stedfastly in the apostles' doctrine and fellowship" (Acts 2:42). Basic to the early Christians' fellowship was their communion with the Lord, which found expression in their relationships one with the other. The types of disorders such as prevailed at Corinth fractured the fellowship of Christians and did a disservice to the good name of the church. Some of the irregularities among the Corinthians occurred in their church gatherings and worship. To encourage that worship among the Corinthians be according to what was proper and orderly, Paul addressed himself to two problems in chapter 11.

The first was the matter of women wearing veils in worship. In no way did Paul deny women the right to be worship leaders. He did insist that when they prayed or prophesied (preached), they wear a head-covering, while he was equally insistent that the men should not. He placed a heavy burden on both men and women to preserve the order of the church.

The problem of women worshiping unveiled, as meat offered to idols, reflects a custom that is no longer in existence—at least not in the Western world. While in our society women do not wear veils, what Paul wrote about the custom cannot be marked off as irrelevant now. The principles on which this argument rest are eternal, and his appeal to modesty are still applicable to this modern day. From Paul's discussion of women wearing veils, a number of truths (as applicable now as in the first century) stand out:

(1) *Distinctions between the sexes should be maintained.* God created male and female. The differences between men and women are rooted in creation itself. A woman's behavior should naturally be different from that of a man. Men and women are to share in public worship, but men should look like men and women should look like women. To avoid the obliteration of distinctions between male and female at Corinth, Paul advised the men to cut their hair and women to cover their heads. The real issue was not the wearing of veils as such, but the maintenance of the divine order of the sexes.

(2) *The husband should be the head of his family.* This was established at creation. Christ is the head (source) of man, and man is the head (source) of woman (Gen. 2). While men and women in Christ are spiritually equal, this provides no basis for changing the social order that God ordained from the beginning. Woman was taken out of man. Man comes through the woman. Each owes his existence to the other (v. 12). Man and woman were made to be partners—made for one another. They are to be a mutual blessing and comfort, not one a slave and the other a tyrant. Nevertheless, God has appointed woman to be man's helper. This does not imply dishonor, for woman is subordinate to her husband as man is subordinate to Christ. The happiest families are those in which God is honored and the husband is the head.

(3) *Flouting customs that are not evil in themselves can have an adverse effect on the Gospel and the Church.* It is wiser to fall in line with harmless conventions than to put a stumbling block in the way of others and bring reproach on the Gospel and the Church.

(4) *Public worship is not an occasion for a style show.* Wearing apparel or mode of dress does, in some measure, reflect the life and character of the worshiper. Men and women are to worship God according to His character and theirs. Daring styles can offend others and detract from the worship of God. Even in small matters, care should be taken to edify the church.

As if the scandal of immodesty among the Corinthians was not enough to cloud the atmosphere of worship in the church, to make matters worse, their conduct—quibbling, gluttony, and even drunkenness—at the Communion service was a disgrace. Such was brought from their love feasts into the celebration of the Lord's Supper. From every indication, the Corinthians did not understand the true character of the Supper. What Paul wrote in seeking to correct their irregularities at the Supper made clear some truths that are relevant today.

(1) *Christians are united with Christ and with one another.* The irregularities, as were common at Corinth, deny the unity of the church and the very spirit of worship. There is no spirit of fellowship where some despise other Christians because of their social and economic standing or for any other reason. Genuine worship is reverent and edifying to all.

(2) *The proper celebration of the Supper affirms the character of Christ.* The Supper proclaims His death, the supreme manifestation of God's love, and points to the time when He will come again. If love is not the effectual force in the gathering of believers around the Lord's table, then the ordinance is empty and has no value.

When the Corinthians came together in a spirit that insulted other believers and offended the Lord, they did not eat the Lord's Supper but their own. Under those conditions it was impossible to eat a true Supper of the Lord. Their failure was to discern the body of Christ—a fellowship created by the Holy Spirit among those in whose hearts He had shed abroad God's love. To partake truly of the holy meal is to take Christ as Lord, and honor Him by recognizing His presence in other members of the Christian fellowship.

(3) *The Lord's Supper is to be observed until He comes.* Since Scripture does not make it clear, frequency of celebration has been debated. But if a church neglects this very important dimension of worship, it does so to the detriment of the spiritual nourishment and growth of the local congregation. Its celebration should be encouraged.

(4) *Spiritual preparation is vital to participation in worship.* The Lord's Supper is no exception. The worshiper is to examine himself so that his worship at the Lord's table is sincere and reverent. Worship is always a serious matter, but all believers need to participate in the Communion service for their spiritual edification when opportunity is given.

CHAPTER 7

THE USE OF SPIRITUAL GIFTS IN WORSHIP
(Chapters 12 and 14)

Three questions were raised in reference to worship at Corinth. The first concerned the place and dress of women; the second regarded the manner of the observance of the Lord's Supper; and the third dealt with the use of spiritual gifts in public worship (12:1—14:40).[1] Chapters 12 and 14 treat the last of these subjects—the use of spiritual gifts.[2]

Paul discussed the subject of spiritual gifts in three particular passages: 1 Corinthians 12-14; Romans 12; and Ephesians 4. His emphasis in these passages falls on the unity of the Spirit, the diversity of the gifts, and the proper use of the gifts in all humility to accomplish their intended purpose.[3] If the catalog of gifts that appears in each of the passages (1 Cor. 12:8-10; Rom. 12:6-8; Eph. 4:11) is compared, differences as well as similarities

---

[1] The writer is aware that 1 Corinthians 13 is an integral part of the discussion of the spiritual gifts in chapters 12 and 14. Because of the fundamental importance of love to the Christian life, the next chapter is devoted to 1 Corinthians 13, which, to say the least, makes good sense as a unit complete in itself.

[2] Spiritual gifts are divine enablements or endowments for worship and service. These are bestowed by the indwelling Holy Spirit and are beyond the natural powers and acquired talents of those through whom they operate. But, in some instances, they may be coupled with natural abilities.

[3] The essential purpose of the gifts of the Spirit is the edification or building up of the Church. The edifying of the Christian community can be understood to include the

become apparent. The most extended treatment that Paul gave of spiritual gifts is found in 1 Corinthians 12-14.

At Corinth, the members of the church had been generously blessed with the gifts of the Spirit. In 1 Corinthians 1:7, Paul said to the church—"You do not lack any spiritual gift" (*NIV*). Their exuberance for exercising the gifts was beyond question, but they had little understanding of their nature and purpose. As a result, the Corinthians' use of the spiritual gifts got out of hand and disrupted good order. Because their worship service was chaotic, it was necessary for Paul to give some instructions as to how gifts could be used for the glory of God. As well as being corrective, his instructions offered directives for Christian worship and for service of the Lord.

THE UNITY OF THE SPIRIT

The church was essentially a worshiping community where the lordship of Christ was acclaimed and the Holy Spirit worked. It was in their church gatherings that a number of the Corinthians' problems centered. One of these problems had to do with the exercise of spiritual gifts.

The Fundamental Test: the Lordship of Jesus (12:1-3). The apostle desired to correct the Corinthians' understanding of spiritual gifts. Before they became Christians, he reminded them, they had been led astray into idolatry. They had worshiped idols, and they had been carried away at moments, by demonic spirits, into frenzy and enthusiasm. On those occasions, they had witnessed

---

addition of members through evangelistic efforts, as well as the enhancement of worship and commitment to the Christian life. The catalog of gifts in Ephesians 4 speaks to this point and consists of apostles, prophets, evangelists, pastors, and teachers. Paul said these were given "for the perfecting of the saints, for the work of the ministry, for the edifying of the body of Christ" (v. 12). The fact that evangelist is included in that list indicates the evangelistic efforts were seen as contributing to the edification of the Church.

manifestations, such as prophecy and speaking in tongues, which reminded them of the gifts of the Spirit as exercised in the Corinthian church; but they were counterfeit gifts (cf. 2 Cor. 11:14-15).

How could the Corinthians know the genuine from the counterfeit? Was there a measure by which they could distinguish the work of the Holy Spirit from religious excitement inspired by evil spirits? According to Paul, there was one fundamental test for the Spirit: No one under the influence of the Holy Spirit could cry, "Jesus is cursed"; but, on the other hand, no one could say, "Jesus is Lord," except by the Holy Spirit.[4] God's Spirit inspired the hearts of individuals to acclaim Jesus as Lord. Anyone could hypocritically call Jesus "Lord" (Matt. 7:21-23), but only by the Holy Spirit could one genuinely accept Christ's authority and proclaim himself a servant of the One whom he confessed as Lord. The confession of Jesus' lordship was a sure sign of the presence and work of the Holy Spirit. The Spirit taught the believers at Corinth to say one thing—"Jesus is Lord."

The lordship of Jesus Christ was, and still is, a measure of whether spiritual gifts are genuine or not. No man can deny His lordship and, at the same time, be directed by the Holy Spirit (John 16:13-15). The Spirit testifies to Christ's reign as Lord. Any worship that does otherwise is not led of the Holy Spirit.

The Unity of Gifts (1 Cor. 12:4-11). The church at Corinth had been blessed with many gifts, but each of them had been

---

[4] The Christian should test the teaching of those who claim to exercise spiritual gifts. Three basic tests are set forth in God's Word: (1) Is their teaching in harmony with the revealed will of God? Since God's will is revealed in Scripture, it is imperative that the Christian know the Bible. Satan can cite Scripture in a deceptive manner (Matt. 4:5-7). (2) Is their teaching faithful to the Biblical view of Christ? See 1 John 4:1-3. (3) What are the fruits of their teachings and what is the effect on those who advocate them? See Matthew 17:15-20.

bestowed by the Holy Spirit. There were varieties of gifts,[5] but they all proceeded from the same Spirit. There were varieties of ministries, but the same Lord (Christ). There were many operations of the gifts, but the same God (Father) who worked them in every believer.[6] The variety of gifts was due to the one Spirit, the one Lord, and the one God.

The triune God was working in the church, but all of the gifts came from the Holy Spirit. The Spirit manifested Himself by the distribution of these gifts to the church. Yet the gifts were ministries in the service of the Lord. They were also operations, behind which stood the power of God.[7] There was a variety of gifts, but their unity was attributable to the triune God.

Each member of the Corinthian church had received a gift appropriate to himself. Equally true was the fact that no gift had been given for private use but for the good of others—for the

---

[5] Paul used two terms for the spiritual gifts that are worth noting at this point. The word *charisma* (*charismata*, "gifts of grace") has both a broad and a restrictive meaning. When used in the broad sense, it has no reference to what we conceive to be spiritual gifts. According to Romans 6:23, "The wages of sin is death; but the gift (*charisma*) of God is eternal life." Too, in Romans 11:29 where Paul referred to God's dealing with Israel, he said the gifts (*charismata*) and calling of God were irrevocable. But Paul also used the term with limited meaning to refer to the gifts of the Spirit. An example is 1 Corinthians 1:7, where he reminded the church that they were not lacking in any gift (*charisma*). This ties directly to Paul's discussion of the gifts in chapters 12-14. The particular word *charisma* indicates the result of action that finds its ground in God's grace (*charis*). The second term for the spiritual gifts in its plural form is *pneumatica*. It appears that in Paul's thought this term is interchangeable with *charismata*. Chapter 12 of 1 Corinthians opens with "Now concerning spiritual gifts" (*pneumatica*) and closes with "but covet earnestly the best gifts" (*charismata*). While the words are used interchangeably, the emphasis in each of them appears to be different. The term *charismata* draws attention to God's grace, which is bestowed in the form of some gift or gifts. The term *pneumatica* directs attention to the Holy Spirit as the donor of the gifts.

[6] *Ministry* is a better rendering of *diakonia* than *administration*.

[7] The three terms—*gifts, ministries,* and *operations*—should not be distinguished one from the other. On the basis of these terms some have construed a threefold classification of the gifts of the Spirit, but responsible research offers no support for such. The variety of terms gives rhetorical effect rather than fine distinctions in meaning; that is, Paul was not setting forth three types of manifestations of the Spirit.

profit of the Christian community. The gifts were not given for the glory of any individual but for the good of the local church. Paul summed it up well: "Now to each one the manifestation of the Spirit is given for the common good" (v. 7 *NIV*). So, with a view toward the building up of the church as a whole, the Spirit bestowed on one a word of wisdom; another, a word of knowledge; another, faith; another, prophecy; another, the ability to distinguish between the spirits; another, various kinds of tongues; and another, the interpretation of tongues.[8] All of these were the working of the same Spirit who freely conferred them on whom He wished.[9] It was His decision as to what gift or gifts

---

[8] Likely the order of the gifts in 1 Corinthians 12 is literary. If a writer desired to call attention to the elements of a broad subject, and then limit the discussion to a few of the elements, he listed last the ones on which he was to elaborate; thus prophecy, tongues, and interpretation of tongues were the focus of Paul's concern in chapters 12 and 14. Furthermore, a comparison of the catalogs of spiritual gifts (1 Cor. 12:8-10; Rom. 12:6-8; Eph. 4:11) reveals that the order is quite fluid. There is just one standard by which the relative importance of gifts is to be determined; that is, whether they bear witness to Jesus Christ as Lord—or, whether they edify the Church.

[9] On whom are the gifts of the Spirit bestowed? Are they given to individuals or to the Church? Some have taken the position that the Holy Spirit has bestowed them on the corporate body, the Church, and that on particular occasions He dispenses them through who He chooses at the time. Others have insisted that Paul clearly stated that the gifts are bestowed on individual Christians—to one is given a word of wisdom and to another a word of knowledge, and so on (1 Cor. 12:8-10). Likely, the truth lies somewhere between the two. It is difficult to give definitive answers to all questions related to this matter of spiritual gifts. But it is clear that some of them issued into a ministry such as "teaching" (12:28) and lifestyles (singleness, 7:7). Paul instructed the one who spoke in tongues to remain silent if no interpreter was present (14:28), and he spoke of certain ones as prophets (12:28). How can a person be known to exercise the gift of interpretation unless he is regularly used to interpret? Or be designated a prophet unless he is give prophetic utterances on a number of occasions? However, this provides no legitimate basis for thinking that one can control, manipulate, and turn a gift off and on at will, nor for the extravagant claim of some that they have all of the gifts. The gifts are to be exercised under the direction of the Holy Spirit, not at the whimsy of any person, and they are distributed throughout the body of Christ. A gift or gifts are granted to a believer because he is a member of the body of Christ. First Corinthians 12, Romans 12, and Ephesians 4 emphasize the place of the gifts in the body. Therefore, it may be said that spiritual gifts are given to the body of Christ and mediated through individual Christians for the benefit of the Church.

each was to receive for the spiritual profit of the entire church. Thus the design of the great variety of gifts was to promote the strength and unity of the Christian community.

The Diversity of Gifts (vv. 12-26). To stress diversity within unity, the apostle used the beautiful picture of the Church as a living body. Although a human body has various parts, each has its own function; and all are vital to the life of the one body. The Church, like the human body, is composed of many members. Each has its place and use, and each is necessary to the welfare of the whole.

So the Church is a unity like a body. The unity of the body of Christ stems from the ministry of the Holy Spirit: "For by one Spirit are we all baptized into one body" (v. 13). This is a reference to water baptism—a sign of the New Birth. By the renewing of the Holy Spirit, all Christians are made members of the body of Christ. Regardless of their nationality (Jew or Gentile) or social standing (slave or free), through that mutual experience they are made spiritually one and united to the body of Christ. Moreover, they are given the one Spirit as drink, and He takes up residence within each of them.

Paul's purpose for using the picture of the body had to do with the life of the Corinthian congregation. The members of that church had not learned to live as a body. There were cliques and divisions within the church (1 Cor. 1:10; 11:18). Some were conceitedly proud of their gifts and exalted them at the expense of the gifts of others. Spiritual gifts were used to promote competition rather than cooperation and unity.

The absurdity of this was clear. Diversities do not cause splits in the human body. The arm is not jealous of the foot, nor does the ear desire to do the smelling. A foot is as much a part of the body as a hand. An ear belongs to the body as much as an eye. God put members in the body as it pleased Him. If all the members were the same, there would be no body. Observe here two dangers:

(1) *Taking one part for the whole (vv. 17-20).* The foot nor the ear is the whole body. The ear cannot do the talking nor the hand the walking. It pleased God that it should be that way for the human body, and the same is true for the body of Christ. God wills variety in the Church.

(2) *Thinking that some members are not needed by the others (vv. 21-22).* No member can dispense with the other. Every member, no matter how weak, is necessary. The small glands of the body are delicate and invisible and certainly are not as strong as the feet and the hands. While they are less honorable because their functions are concealed, they are no less vital to the body than the visible members.

In placing the members in the body, God intended that none should be despised. The basis for this was twofold:

(1) *The less attractive members are adorned with finer attire and on them is bestowed special honor.* Certain parts of the human body are unseemly. These are not held in contempt, nor is it felt that they are not needed. Modesty demands that they be clothed; thus, the unseemly members are given a greater seemliness. The Corinthians were esteeming one member over another, but the weaker and humbler members of the church should not have been despised. That was not the way God treated them. He tempered the difference by bestowing on them "more abundant honor." The arrangement of the church was not due to chance but to God's ordering. What He did secured a general equality and blended the members of the church together into a harmonious whole.

(2) *There are mutual dependences.* What happens to one organ of a body affects the others. If I break my arm, only the arm is broken; but the pain and inconveniences affect my total self. When a member suffers, all suffer. Let us remember that Paul's concern

here was the Corinthians' use of spiritual gifts. If one member appeared to be deficient in such gifts, the rest of the church was not to despise him. He was not the only sufferer; the whole church suffered. If another seemed to have more than his share of the gifts, he was not to boast nor were the rest to envy him. All were to rejoice in the gifts bestowed on each one. The honor and joy of one were the honor and joy of all. All benefited spiritually.

God created the Church as He did so "there should be no schism in the body; but the members should have the same care one for another" (v. 25). Diversity does not justify divisions. The Corinthians as "the body of Christ" had received a variety of gifts necessary to that body. At the same time, they were to maintain care for one another so the unity of the body would be preserved. But they "had so distorted their diversity into division that congregational unity was seriously imperiled, if not already fractured.[10]

The Mutual Interdependence of Gifts (vv. 27-31). Every member of the church had some service to perform and, thus, had some appropriate gift. The Holy Spirit had distributed in wide and varied ways the gifts among the many members. God himself had set in the church a variety of ministries—apostles, teachers, workers of miracles, gifts of healing, ability to help others, gifts of administration, and speaking in different kinds of tongues. Not all had the same ministry. Not all were apostles, or prophets, or teachers, or administrators, or empowered with the gift of healing or gift of tongues[11] or the gift of interpretation. All of these gift ministries were designed to promote order and unity. Each needed the oth-

---

[10] Spittler, *op. cit.,* p. 63.

[11] Paul asked, "Do all speak with tongues?" The negative (*mē*) that Paul employed makes it clear that the anticipated answer was no. Each of the gifts of the Spirit is designed for the edification of the Church. The gift of tongues is no exception. God does not bestow any of the gifts on all believers. So all do not speak in tongues for the edification of the Church, but all who are baptized in the Spirit may speak in tongues (devotional) for their own personal edification.

er, and each complemented the other. The spiritual growth and health of the church depended on each doing what he could.

THE GIFTS IN WORSHIP

The apostle opened chapter 14 with the recognition of the primacy of love ("Follow the way of love") as he closed chapter 12 ("I will show you the most excellent way," *NIV*). Coupled with these was the admonition to covet or desire earnestly (*zeloute,* "eagerly desire," 14:1; 12:31) spiritual gifts. This depicted what the Corinthian believers were to do by the power of the Spirit. As well as pursuing love, all were to strive zealously for spiritual gifts because God had made them available. Paul gave some guidelines for use of the vocal gifts so that the Corinthians would regulate them in the interest of orderly worship and the edification of the church.

Prophecy and Speaking in Tongues (14:1-25). Like all the gifts, speaking in tongues was a good gift from God, but the Corinthians tended to exalt this gift out of proportion. Too, the exercise of tongues without interpretation had created confusion in their worship. At this point, a distinction may be made between what has been described as "devotional tongues" and the gift of tongues. *Devotional tongues,* which is proper for all Spirit-baptized believers, edifies only the speaker and is intended more for private than public worship. The *gift of tongues* is given for public use and demands interpretation so the local church may be edified.[12] Only when tongues are accompanied by interpretation do they profit the entire congregation.

Evidently, the Corinthians did not understand that edification of the church was the true aim of the gifts. Tongues without interpretation were common in their worship services. This

---

[12] This raises the question of the directional nature of tongues (*glossolalia*); that is, does speaking in tongues bear character of a message to man or does all glossolalia bear the character of prayer and praise to God? It is the view of this writer that glossolalia is not exclusively prayer and praise. Paul admonished the one who spoke in tongues to pray for interpretation (14:13). Does this not assume a message directed to the people?

was disruptive rather than edifying. Since often there was no interpretation of tongues in their services, only the speaker was edified; for he spoke to God, not to men. Only God understood what he said. In his own spirit he uttered mysteries.

Though his spirit was directly influenced by the Holy Spirit, his speaking was an activity of his spirit but not of his understanding. Paul said later, "If I pray in a tongue, my spirit prays, but my mind is unfruitful" (v. 14 NIV). No one but the speaker was edified. Since edification of the entire church was the main goal, uninterpreted tongues were not to be used in group worship. If no one present could provide an interpretation, the speaker was to keep quiet in the church and speak to himself and God (v. 28).

Uninterpreted tongues were uncertain. On the other hand, a message of prophecy[13] was given in the language of the hearers, and its meaning was clear. So, the gift of prophecy was greater because it offered edification, exhortation, and comfort to the church. But tongues had a place of importance and real value in corporate worship when accompanied by the gift of interpretation. This gift had the effect of turning tongues into edification for the entire local church.

The Corinthians knew Paul intended to visit them. If he came to Corinth speaking in tongues, how would that benefit and uplift the local church unless he brought some revelations, knowledge, prophecy, or teaching? Only by the interpretation of tongues could the Corinthians benefit comparably to Paul's speaking by the way of revelation, knowledge, prophecy, or teaching.

Unless tongues were interpreted, their meaning was uncertain. To illustrate this point, a flute or harp produces a melody according to the law of harmony. If it makes no distinct tone,

---

[13] In the early church prophecy on occasions consisted of prediction, but exhortation and exposition of Christian truth were the more common elements.

there is confusion. Again, if a bugle does not sound clearly, the soldiers know not what to do—whether to prepare for war or to come for roll call.

Through an interpreter, tongues were valuable for the worshiping church. Otherwise, a Christian, to be understood, had to speak intelligibly or else talk to the wind. There were many languages in the world, but no one could know them all. If a person was not understood, he appeared to those present as a foreigner and what he said sounded like mere babbling. To avoid this, Paul exhorted those zealous to have spiritual gifts to seek them for the building up of the church. One who spoke in tongues was to pray for the gift to interpret so he might be understood by all the worshipers.

It is not stated exactly how tongues, coupled with interpretation, served to edify the church, but it can be assumed that the Corinthians' faith was stimulated and strengthened as they heard the things of God in their language. However, uninterpreted tongues tended to break down, rather than to build up the church. This was why Paul preferred to speak a few words in an intelligible language than ten thousand words in a tongue (v. 19).

On some occasions, tongues manifested among the Corinthian believers took the form of praying or of singing. With this in mind, Paul spoke, on the one hand, of praying in a tongue and praying with the spirit and, on the other hand, of singing with the spirit (vv. 14-15).[14] Praying and singing in tongues had their place, but the mind of the speaker was unfruitful. An understanding of speaking in tongues was only possible by interpretation. If one gave thanks in tongues, how could another, who found himself among those who did not understand, say amen? The thanksgiving might have been excellent, but the person unable

---

[14] These verses do not necessarily indicate that the usual content of glossolalia was prayer and thanksgiving but often might have included words of praise and blessing to God.

to respond was not edified. To serve the interests of others, it was necessary for thanksgiving offered in tongues to be interpreted. The gift of tongues was good. No doubt, Paul would not have been disobedient to the leading of the Holy Spirit to minister any gift; but unless interpretation was provided for tongues, he preferred to speak in public worship a known tongue.

While it was not Paul's purpose to discredit the manifestation of the gift of tongues in corporate worship, he felt that the Corinthians had exalted it at the expense of other gifts. For them it was a mark (perhaps, *the* mark) of God's favor. Being aware of their immaturity in the matter of spiritual gifts, he appealed to them to use their heads in an adult fashion and to make mature Christian judgments.

As already noted, tongues plus interpretation edified the church (vv. 5, 12). But there was another purpose; namely, they served as a sign to the unbelievers. The gift was exercised to impress unbelievers, but that did not necessarily mean this would convert them. It may be inferred that the condemnation of those who rejected the sign was increased. This was Paul's point when he cited Isaiah 28:11 to support his contention that tongues were to be used as a sign for unbelievers. The prophet Isaiah had told disobedient Israel that since they refused to listen to his words, God would speak to them with strange tongues and the lips of foreigners. When the Assyrians invaded Palestine, their foreign speech was a sign of impending doom for God's rebellious people. Therefore, Paul maintained that the gift of tongues in the church called the unbelieving and hardhearted to God. Tongues with interpretation were a sign of God's presence to influence unbelievers.

The crux of the matter is stated in verse 23: "If therefore the whole church be come together into one place, and all speak with tongues, and there come in those that are unlearned, or unbelievers, will they not say that ye are mad [*mainesthe*]?" Did Paul identify speaking in tongues with madness? It must be noticed what the apostle said: "If . . . *all* speak with tongues . . . ye [plural] are mad." These words were directed against all, at one time or in rapid succession, speaking in tongues, with the clear implication that no interpretation was given. Under such conditions, the charge of madness could have been brought against the Corinthians. No doubt, if the whole church spoke in tongues without interpretations, the unbelievers present would have thought them to be out of their wits.

But prophecy, which was a sign to believers, would bring the unbeliever under conviction. He would more readily be convicted through prophecy than through uninterrupted tongues. He would be brought face-to-face with God and with his spiritual condition. His heart would be probed. Falling on his face, he would worship God and report that God was among them.

Orderly Worship (vv. 26-33, 39-40). The apostle urged the Corinthians to preserve order within the diverse ministries of the Spirit. To argue this matter, he provided a picture of a Corinthian worship service, which was likely typical of such occasions throughout the early church.

The main feature was that each could take part in the service. Anyone who had a gift had the opportunity to exercise it. One had a hymn inspired by the Holy Spirit (Eph. 5:19; Col. 3:16). Another was able to expound doctrine to teach "even the words of our Lord Jesus Christ, and . . . the doctrine which is according to godliness" (1 Tim. 6:3). Yet another had a revelation, a divine truth, especially relating to salvation or to the Second Coming. Still another had the gift of tongues, while another had the gift of interpretation. The members of the Corinthian church had at their disposal a variety of spiritual gifts. Each was to have a chance to exercise his gift, but all was to be used for the upbuilding of the church.

To stress the importance of this, Paul laid down a fundamental principle that ruled out anything that would disturb good order in public worship: "Let all things be done unto edifying" (1 Cor. 14:26). As to the use of tongues, he specified that no more than three speakers at the most should be heard at a service of worship. The apparent reason for this limitation was that spiritual eruptions were not to become so numerous as to usurp the reading of Scripture and its normal exposition. When there was an utterance in tongues, it was to be followed by interpretation. If no interpreter was recognized to be present, he was to remain silent or speak inaudibly—"let him speak to himself, and to God" (v. 28).

It is clear from this and other regulations that speaking in tongues was not an uncontrollable exercise.[15] The Christian who felt moved to speak in tongues had the ability, if it was so warranted, to restrain the impulse. What was said of the prophets could be equally true of those who exercised the gifts of tongues— "The spirits of the prophets are subject to the prophets" (v. 32). Contrary to what some of the Corinthians believed, no one was to think of tongues as the irresistible result of the Spirit's driving man into utterance.

Prophecy was also subject to regulation. Not more than two or three prophets were to speak, while others were to consider carefully what was said (v. 29). Those who possessed the gift of discernment were to decide whether the prophets' utterances really came from God. The message of a prophet was not to be given uncritical acceptance but was to be tested by those qualified. Those who wanted to speak were to control the impulse in deference to one another—only one speaking at a time—so "that all may learn, and all may be comforted" (v. 31). No one could truthfully say he was so carried away in the Spirit that he could not control himself. Without quenching the Spirit, the

---

[15] Paul's teaching makes it clear that glossolalia is not ecstatic in nature. This gift is exercised under the individual's control. He does not speak involuntarily nor is he irrational, but he is responsible for maintaining order as the gift is exercised through him. The speaker is possessed of the Spirit, yet master of his own spirit.

prophets, as well as those who had gifts of tongues, could control their spirits. God was not a God of confusion.

The exercise of both tongues and prophecy was regulated by the apostle. It should not be forgotten that the purpose for his imposing limitations on speaking in tongues was not to discredit the manifestation of this important gift in the worship services, but to show the Corinthians, who viewed it as the gift *par excellence*, its relative value when compared with the other gifts, especially prophecy. He did restrict the public exercise of the gift of tongues, but he recognized its value in building up the church. He said, "Do not forbid speaking in tongues" and "I would like every one of you to speak in tongues" (vv. 39, 5 *NIV*). Not only this, but he said, "I thank God that I speak in tongues more than all of you" (v. 18 *NIV*). Nor did he question the genuineness of utterances in tongues, for he said of uninterpreted tongues, "You are giving thanks well enough" (v. 17 *NIV*). Moffatt summarizes well Paul's attitude toward the gift of tongues:

> *He values the gift as something not only good but exalted; it is a divine manifestation of the Spirit, not a hallucination. He admits that it is something to be coveted (xiv. 1-5, 39). He himself is proud of having the gift, and he never dreams of doubting the reality of an inspired ecstasy which he knew from experience to be authentic.*[16]

CONCLUSION

The life of the church is its worship. To neglect it or the maintenance of proper order in it can be devastating. Paul's exposition of the spiritual gifts shows their fundamental importance in the meetings of the Church and to Christian experience. According to the Biblical view, the gifts are to have a servant role and those through whom they work are to be servants. God has given the gifts of administration, pastoring,

---

[16] James Moffatt, *The First Epistle of Paul to the Corinthians*, p. 211.

teaching, evangelizing, and all the others, not to exalt those who have a gift, but that these people might serve and build up the body of Christ. There is a place for every believer's gift. The lay membership has a vital place, as does the ministry. Some have this gift; others have that gift. Each is to exercise his special gift or gifts, at the same time respecting all the others. To prefer one gift over another and to belittle certain gifts is not proper. God can use them all if they are consecrated to His service and to the edifying of the Church.

As it had become at Corinth, worship can be divisive because of overexuberance for certain spiritual gifts, which results in their exercise without any restraint. The call is made for order and unity in worship rather than for uniformity. The Holy Spirit knits the church together, and His diverse gifts empower it and determine its duties. There is to be mutual recognition of ministries so that no single gift is given precedence as the Corinthians did tongues. All the gifts are essential to the life of the Christian community.

Pentecostals have rightly emphasized that the church is the place where the Holy Spirit works. There must be freedom for Him to move, but He is never the source of confusion and disorder. A worship service can be so rigidly structured that it stifles or enslaves the Spirit. But structure can also aid the Spirit; with no structure, there is a chaotic situation. The key to balance and order in worship is a structure that allows for freedom and spontaneity.[17] Where these are found, at times the leader in worship may stand back from the place of leadership in worship and recognize the special leadership provided by the divine presence.

Corporate worship in which spontaneity and order are united provides the best conditions for the Holy Spirit to move and to

---

[17] Oscar Cullmann, *Early Christian Worship*, p. 33, states well the compatibility between spontaneity and order in the worship of the early church when he says, "It is precisely in this harmonious combination of freedom and restriction that there lies the greatness and uniqueness of the early Christian service of worship."

distribute His gifts. These gifts enhance the awareness of the Lord's presence and glorify God's wisdom and knowledge, His faithfulness and power. Where the gifts are bestowed, the Lord is recognized as being in the midst. The manifestation of any one of the spiritual gifts is supremely a revelation of God. It points— like the hand of John the Baptist—to the Lord among His people and is evidence of His powerful presence in a congregation. As a result, Spirit-filled worshipers celebrate and respond to the Lord in the midst of His worshiping church. By the Holy Spirit, they declare that Jesus is Lord.

Such balance in worship was absent among the Corinthian believers. They exercised the gifts in a spontaneous manner; but the result was utter confusion in their meetings, making true worship impossible. There was a tendency among them to overemphasize the gifts of tongues. Many have felt that contemporary Pentecostals are guilty of the same, but the fact is that they give no more prominence to speaking in tongues than the New Testament does, since it is so prominent. Out of all the gifts, speaking in tongues was the sign on the Day of Pentecost and at the Gentile Pentecost (Acts 2:4; 10:46).

The Corinthians could have been commended for their spiritual fervor, but spiritual fervor is never enough. If carried to excess, it creates disorder. God is never the source of confusion. As is seen in the material world, God is the author of law, order, and decorum and thus conducts the affairs of the church accordingly. Regulation of spiritual gifts in worship recommended by Paul does not stifle the Spirit's working in the lives of gifted people; but it does stress the importance of the preservation of order so the entire assembly may be edified. An uncontrolled and uncontrollable prophet is not genuine nor Biblical, for the Spirit permits a prophet control over his spirit so there is no uncontrolled speaking that results in disorder. As far as the manner of public worship of God goes, Paul's words are always apt: "Let all things be done decently and in order" (1 Cor. 14:40)

CHAPTER 8

THE WAY OF REDEMPTIVE LOVE
(12:31—13:13)

Christian love is "the greatest thing in the world." But *love* is a word with several meanings. It is important to understand the way the term is used in 1 Corinthians 13.

There are at least two Greek words that are translated into English as *love*. One is the word *eros*, which often expresses the desire to possess or enjoy its object and so to obtain satisfaction and self-fulfillment. It is essentially selfish and seeks to use people for its own pleasure. This word is not used in the New Testament. The other word is *agapē*, which in 1 Corinthians 13 the King James Version renders *charity*. The kind of love that is often expressed by this word aims to give pleasure and satisfaction to the object of its affection. It desires to help rather than to possess and enjoy its object. It does not merely love the lovable but also the unlovable and unlovely. It is fundamentally unselfish and seeks the good of the beloved. Of course, this does not mean the lover gets no pleasure out of sharing his love. His satisfaction grows out of his giving to others and his sharing in their joy.

The kind of love shown by God is *agapē*. It is the love of John 3:16, which describes the great sacrificial outpouring of God's heart for His rebellious children. The revelation of divine love has given us a glimpse into the personal character of God. The idea of love as giving is bound up with God's disclosure of Himself. "God commendeth his love toward us, in that, while we were yet sinners, Christ died for us" (Rom. 5:8; cf. 1 John 4:10). God's love is concerned with the welfare of the undeserving and confers blessings on those who have no right to them nor show any love to Him.

Believers know themselves to be loved in God's loving forgiveness. The love of God is poured out in the hearts of the children of God (Rom. 5:5). It is in His love that their love originates. His love generates in their hearts love for others. Love is *the* mark of the new life in Christ and furnishes the highest standard for Christian conduct.

The Christian flock at Corinth had failed miserably in the practice of love. There were factions and carnality; there were lawsuits among the believers; there was the self-centered practice of Christian liberty; there was the perversion of the Lord's Supper. In their worldly self-seeking, the Corinthians abused the use of the spiritual gifts.

It was precisely in love that the gifts were to be exercised. Love does not displace the gifts, but this fruit of the Spirit[1] is the regulative principle behind the gifts of the Spirit and is the spirit in which gifts must be used. Love is not jealous or boastful but is patient and kind, giving other members endowed with the Spirit an opportunity to exercise their gifts.

"But covet earnestly the best gifts: and yet shew I unto you a more excellent way" (12:31). "Follow after charity [love],

---

[1] Love is not classified by Paul as one of the gifts of the Spirit but as a fruit. The description of love in 1 Corinthians 13:4-7 is remarkably parallel to the fruit of the Spirit in Galatians 5:22-23: love, joy, peace, long-suffering, goodness, faithfulness, meekness, and self-control. These are not "gifts" in the narrow sense as they are really an expression of Christian character. The Holy Spirit is the source and substance of love's power in the believer's life. It is the natural consequence of a life lived in the Spirit.

and desire spiritual gifts" (14:1).[2] This "more excellent way" is described in the song of praise[3] in chapter 13; it is the way of redemptive love.

THE PREEMINENCE OF REDEMPTIVE LOVE

God's love is the governing principle of the Christian life and the highway of holiness that leads to that everlasting city. It is the true motive for living and for the use of the spiritual gifts—in fact, for all ministry. The song of love opens with a solemn warning that makes it clear that love working with the spiritual gifts is the more excellent way.

Love Is Better Than the Tongues of Men and Angels (1 Cor. 13:1). The reference, it seems, was made to the gift of tongues, which the Corinthians had abused; but "men and angels" imply a contrast between earth and heaven. Paul himself spoke of hearing "unspeakable words, which it is not lawful for a man to utter" (2 Cor. 12:4) when he was "caught up to the third heaven" (v. 2). So "tongues of angels" possibly refers to speaking languages higher than human languages. What Paul meant was the most eloquent and exalted speaking. All such speaking, apart from love, does not bless and edify others.

If a loveless believer speaks in tongues, he has passed over a vital matter—*love*, the essential ingredient of any gift. The exercise of his gift has little influence on the congregation. He is

---

[2] Observe that Paul put down in the middle of his discussion of the spiritual gifts the song of praise to love. Where did Paul get this hymn of praise to love? It must have been based on the life of Jesus Christ and provides a description of His character. Christ's lifestyle determined Paul's understanding of love. The name *Jesus* could be substituted for *love (agapē)* in 1 Corinthians 13. Paul had experienced the transforming love of God. So he wrote out of his religious experience and his knowledge of the life of his Lord.

[3] Paul did not belittle any spiritual gift nor did he suggest the gifts were not genuine when they were being used in the interest of competition and display rather than for the edification of the church. Those who used the gifts without love were nothing—not their gifts. The deficiency was not in the gifts but in individuals endowed with the gifts.

only "as sounding brass, or a tinkling cymbal" (13:1) if he lacks love—indeed, nothing more than a loud noise. The church is not moved by such but left dead and cold. If the man has love in his heart, his speaking in tongues, coupled with interpretation edifies others.

Love Is Better Than the Gifts of Prophecy, Knowledge, and Faith (v. 2). A Christian may have the prophetic gift and thus be able to foretell future events or to preach the Word of God with great skill but have no real love for the congregation. He may fill an important pulpit and be hailed by many as the shining light in the church. What he says may be true, but it is not said in love. His motivation is not love but frustration and disappointment, which he may vent by dangling his people over coals of fire. Regardless of how great his prophetic powers are, he is nothing without love.

Another Christian may have a knowledge of all the mysteries of revelation (Rom. 11:25, 33; 16:25-26; Eph. 3:1-10) and a mental grasp of all intellectual knowledge. This is a rare combination—the mystic insight of a prophet joined with the intellect of a philosopher. A man devoid of redeeming love may become inflated over his insight or learning. Spiritual insight not blended with love can make a man a spiritual snob. Intellectual achievement not inspired by love can make a man an intellectual snob. God does not need the ignorance of any man, but insight and learning without love may result in pride and cold detachment. If one knows everything there is to know and has no love, he is nothing. A deep understanding is of no value without a charitable heart.

Still another Christian may have "all faith" so that he can work miracles. Possessing faith in its greatest degree, he is able to uproot or tear out mountain after mountain; that is, to make what seems impossible possible. The worker of miracles may amaze the multitudes; but, if love is absent, his mighty works will go for nought. Miracle-working faith void of love will not lead people to the feet of Jesus. Such faith must be merged in love.

Love Is Better Than Personal Sacrifice (1 Cor. 13:3). Benevolent and charitable acts are valueless without a benevolent and charitable heart. Giving away piece by piece all of one's possessions apart from love profits nothing. The one who makes that kind of sacrifice without love has hidden motives, expecting recompense that is not too apparent. He could go so far as to give himself to the most painful ordeals—death by fire. If he has no love, it is no credit to him. To give away all that one has or endure the most cruel suffering, while withholding his heart from God and from others is no profit at all. It is all wasted. Love must prompt and inspire what is done. Otherwise, there is no present blessing or future reward for it.

Paul spoke of "a more excellent way." What is that? It is not just speaking, whether with the tongues of men or angels. It is not merely knowledge—that puffs up. It is not just faith, regardless of its miracle-working strength. It is not merely sacrifice, though all may be given away. "A more excellent way" is speaking in love; it is love coupled with knowledge and understanding; it is love working with faith; it is love motivating sacrifice. The exercise of the gifts with love is the more excellent way. In fact, love puts quality and character into all that a Christian does and is the spirit that enables him or her to have a true spiritual ministry.

THE CHARACTER OF REDEMPTIVE LOVE

Love seeks the best for the other person, but it was never defined by Paul. He did, however, describe its wonderful characteristics, both negatively and positively. As many have, perhaps he, too, found it easier to tell what love does and does not do, than to define it.

What Love Does Not Do. (1) *Love is not envious.* Its very nature desires the well-being of others and maintains a healthy appreciation of them. Love knows no jealousy and has no ill feeling toward those with more ability, more honor, or a greater abundance of this world's goods. Love is not rooted in the neurotic and demonic need to use and dominate others. It is not possessive[4] and never seeks its own—praise, honor, or profit—at the hurt of others. Someone has said that there are two kinds of people in America—the millionaires and those who would like to be. Love never covets and does not desire things for itself as much as it desires things for others.

(2) *Love is not boastful.* It does not put on a display or make a show. Love never toots its own horn. Indeed, it is concerned with doing good to all people, but it does not seek recognition or applause. Though it excels in good works, love is impressed with its unworthiness rather than its merit.

(3) *Love is not proud.* It is never swelled up with pride and self-importance. The person with an oversized self-esteem fills his own little world. In his own eyes, he is one of God's prized specimens, and God is fortunate to have him as a member of His family. Being so full of self, he is a nuisance and hard to get along with. Such is alien to love. For love has no thought of superiority above other Christians, nor is it inflated with self-importance and self-sufficiency.

(4) *Love is not rude.* It has good manners and never forgets courtesy. It does not act discourteously and tactlessly. Politeness is its style. There is a kind of "Christianity" that delights in being

---

[4] There is one exception to this. Married love is possessive and limited. God intended it to be that way. According to His plan, the marriage relationship involves total commitment. "For this cause shall a man leave father and mother, and shall cleave to his wife: and they twain shall be one flesh" (Matt. 19:5-6). The stress falls on oneness of marriage, which calls for love that is expressed in faithfulness to one person. However, even in marriage one does not completely possess another person. Marriage partners are to give themselves to one another, but that does not involve ownership. As Paul indicated, husband and wife do not have absolute rule over their bodies but are to submit willingly to one another (1 Cor. 7:1-5).

blunt and making others uncomfortable. Such is unbecoming to any Christian. If a Christian loves people, he wants them to be comfortable. Jesus was sensitive to people's needs and showed great kindness in dealing with them and their frailties. Politeness and good manners were His style. An ill-mannered Christian has failed to let the Master's style become his own. Good manners, part of the fabric of love, gives style to the Christian faith.

(5) *Love is not self-seeking.* Some people think only of their rights and insist on their own way. This is nothing but selfishness, which often is at the bottom of strife in the home or church. Pushing through one's own claims and carnal self-seeking have no place in love. It never seeks its own advancement, pleasure, and honor at the expense and disregard of others, but it looks to their interest rather than to its own.

(6) *Love does not break out in sudden anger.* It does not become exasperated with people, nor is it at cross-purposes with others. Always keeping its head, love never loses its temper. It remains calm and unruffled when tried, and refuses to be disturbed or distressed by petty things that upset and hurt others deeply. Love puts a charitable construction on what others say and do, being ready to make allowances for their failures and provocations.

(7) *Love keeps no record of wrongs.* The term (*logizomai*) rendered in the King James Version *thinketh* comes from the bookkeeper's profession. It means "to charge to comeone" or "to put to one's credit" and is used for entering an item in a ledger so it will not be forgotten. That is precisely what many people do. At least they keep a mental list of wrongs suffered. It is hard not to remember, but love forgets personal injustices. To forgive is to forget. No one can do this on his own, but Christ can so change one's inner life to make forgiveness and forgetting possible. Love keeps no books on the slights or wrongs received, but covers a multitude of sins (1 Peter 4:8). In short, it knows how to forgive and to forget.

(8) *Love does not rejoice in iniquity.* The word *iniquity* here can be translated *unrighteousness.* Love does not rejoice in the failings and sins of others. The fall of others grieves love. It is concerned with the spiritual welfare of all people and takes no pleasure in the backsliding and moral failures of others. Such brings sorrow to love.

What Love Does Do. (1) *Love suffers long.* Often the word here describes patience with people rather than with circumstances. It takes greater love to be long-suffering toward provoking individuals than it does with disturbing circumstances. A person who has been wronged and has in his power to avenge himself but does not, is an example of long-suffering. That is the way love behaves. It is always slow to anger; it never grows impatient; it never retaliates.

(2) *Love is kind.* A person may be religious and not be kind, but he cannot reflect what a genuine Christian is and not be kind. While persecuting the church, Paul was religious, but he did not know Christ and was not kind. A Christlike Christian is kind, even to those who are unkind to him. He follows the example of Christ, of whom it is written, "Who, when he was reviled, reviled not again; when he suffered, he threatened not" (1 Peter 2:23).

(3) *Love rejoices in the truth*; that is, love seeks the truth. Its joy is not tracking down and pointing out wrong, but witnessing what is true. Love wants truth to prevail and rejoices in the spread and triumph of truth. There may be times when some Christians do not want truth to prevail or do not desire to hear the truth. But love has no desire or need to conceal the truth. It has nothing to hide and so is glad when truth prevails.

(4) *Love bears all things.* The original meaning of the verb *bear* (*stegō*) was "to cover." Since in the immediate context reference is made to the endurance of love, the emphasis may be that love, in a sense, does cover the failings of others; that is, it does

not discuss what is undesirable or sinful in someone else. Love strives to believe in the other person and does not make an issue of his faults or herald abroad his failures.

(5) *Love believes all things.* Should this be interpreted to mean that it is gullible or is easily deceived? Not at all. This would be quite contrary to Paul's teaching about the judgments of spirits and distrust of false prophets. It must refer to the fact that love is full of faith. Regardless of the circumstances, it is always ready to give due credence to others; it does not inject groundless suspicions or question the sincerity of the acts of others. Anything that is not known to be false, love is willing to consider. Indeed, love has a trusting heart and never loses its faith.

(6) *Love endures all things.* With hope in deliverance at the second coming of Christ, love endures trials, persecutions, and hardships. This does not mean that wrong is to be covered up; but in spite of the imperfections of others, love will endure injury, and abuse will not cause it to wane. Love can stand the tests of life and outwear anything.

THE SUPREMACY OF REDEMPTIVE LOVE

Sounding a note of victory, Paul declared, "Love never fails." Love will exist throughout all eternity. It will always have its place and never will it be out of use. Though the gifts of the Spirit will be abolished when God's kingdom comes fully, love never will end. The gifts will not be vital to the resurrected life of the Christians, but love will continue.

Love Holds Supremacy Over the Spiritual Gifts (1 Cor. 13:8-12). The gifts belong to this present world and "will pass away." Prophecy, speaking in tongues, and knowledge will have no part to play in eternity. At the return of Christ, there will be no more prophecy to be foretold and no more to be interpreted or fulfilled. The prediction and exposition of the will of God will have come to an end. For then the total will of God will be known by

133

believers. Consequently, there will be no more need for prophets and prophecy. The same applies to speaking in tongues, which edifies the individual and the church when interpreted. After Christ has come again, tongues will have no useful purpose.

Even knowledge that Christians now possess will have no place upon the arrival of the perfect. It will be abolished, not in the interest of ignorance but of a fuller understanding. "For we know in part, and we prophesy in part. But when that which is perfect is come, then that which is in part shall be done away" (vv. 9-10). Though God gave a perfect revelation in Jesus Christ, believers do not have a perfect grasp of it. At best, they have now only partial knowledge. The future, however, holds a brighter prospect. When the state of perfection is reached, that which is partial and fragmentary will be abolished. When Christ comes for His own, this will become a glorious reality.

Limited earthly understanding and the full grasp of the truth, which is to come, can be likened to the difference between a child and a man. Childish ways are all right for a child, but the talk, thought, and judgment of a child are ill-becoming to a grown man and are laid aside by him. Childish ways are outgrown and are put away in maturity. As a child cannot comprehend the affairs of the adult, the believer, until he arrives at the future state, will not know as God knows him. The word *childish* does carry a note of derision. However, Paul did not deride the gifts, but the Corinthians' perversion of the gifts. Their immaturity led them to overvalue gifts and to undervalue love.

The apostle did not mean that gifts like prophecy, tongues, and knowledge can be dispensed with now by mature Christians. The most mature are but little children in their understanding of the truths and realities of God. Thus, there remains a need for spiritual gifts in this present age. They will cease to be useful when the age of the perfect has fully come, but not until then. In this age of the partial, for which these gifts are designed, the believers' vision is limited. "For now we see only a reflection in a mirror;[5] then we shall see face to face. Now I know in part; then I shall know fully, even as I am fully known" (v. 12 *NIV*).

While Christians live out their lives on this earth, they are, by the Holy Spirit, given only a few rays of truth. Their sight of things eternal is, at best, unclear; they have only a dim reflection of divine realities. But there will be full light in the life to come. For then they will see Christ face-to-face and will know things as the Lord now knows them. The glorified believers will have perfect vision and understanding; they will know as they are known by God.

On the day of the Lord partial knowledge will be abolished; the gifts of the Spirit will have no place. The Christian has now only an imperfect knowledge, but he also possesses something unchangeable, *love*. It occupies the supreme place and will never end.

Love Holds Supremacy Over Faith and Hope (v. 13). Faith, hope, and love will abide forever. It is generally agreed that the verb *abides* (*menei*) here is used with a future sense. While the spiritual gifts will pass away, faith, hope, and love will continue.[6]

It may seem strange to speak of faith and hope as elements of the final state of the Christian. Will faith and hope still have a place and not be superfluous then? In eternity, faith will become sight, and hope will be actual realization. When faith is

---

[5] William Barclay, *Letter to the Corinthians*, p. 139, says, "Corinth was famous for its manufacture of mirrors. The Corinthian mirror was made of highly polished metal. At best, the reflection that it gave was imperfect. The modern mirror with its perfect reflection did not emerge until the thirteenth century."

[6] The other two members of the triad, *faith* and *hope*, are broad spiritual qualities. Such qualities which characterize the believer's present fellowship with God do not necessarily cease at the second coming of Christ. God's everlasting kingdom will not be one of spiritual idleness or devoid of spiritual qualities. The believer's present understanding of these is limited by the fact that he exists in a state in which his salvation is incomplete. No doubt *faith* and *hope* will be redefined in new terms in a way similar to knowledge, which will be abolished by the coming of a wider and nobler intelligence (13:8, 12).

exchanged for sight, the Christian will enter into full salvation and all uncertainty will be done away. So, faith and hope as they have to do with salvation will have no place. But, in another sense, faith and hope will continue.

Faith is the grateful and trustful acceptance of God as He is.[7] God is gracious and will continue to be. Faith is the eternal mark of the true relationship between God and man. That relationship is rooted in divine grace. The recognition and acceptance of the gracious God as He is will always be in order. Faith will abide forever.

Hope is confident assurance that what God has given He will maintain. When the believer no longer sees in a glass, but face-to-face, he will be in full possession of God's gift, on which he has patiently waited. Even then he will continue to put his hope in God. No other than God will be his hope. He will look with serene confidence to God to conserve the gift of eternal life. The believer will always have faith and hope in God, even after he is with his blessed Lord in glory.

All three—faith, hope, and love—are inseparable. All three endure; they are a fact of the present and future condition of the believer. In this regard they are on the same footing. Love will not abide longer than faith and hope. These three are timeless.

Love, however, is superior to faith and hope. Love's companions, faith and hope, are vitally important, but there is nothing greater than love. Without love, those with spiritual gifts, even those with the most confident faith, are nothing. It is love which believes and which hopes. Even as vital as faith and hope are, they are surpassed by love.

Why is love the greatest? It is a property of God. John says, "God is love" (1 John 4:8, 16). God acts by love, not by faith or hope. God does not trust in the sense of putting trust in some

---

[7] Faith here is not the miracle-working faith of verse 2.

other being. He does not hope. He is what He is and what He will be. He has no hope of becoming anything that He is not already. On the other hand, if God did not love, He would not be God. Love holds the supreme place, for it is the essential character of divine activity. Indeed, it is the greatest.

CONCLUSION

The Corinthian church was a Pentecostal church, but it was lacking in love. A church may sing exuberantly, be enthusiastic for spiritual gifts and for their operation, and attract large numbers to its worship services, but be hollow, empty, and devoid of the real essence and substance of the Christian faith, which is love. A church may be hard-working and orthodox, holding to its teachings and declaration of faith, resisting error and affirming the truth in its fellowship and in its community. The members may work hard at their faith. Their involvement in Christian endeavors shows they are not complacent but diligent and faithful. All these may be done without love. If this is the case, the life of that church is hollow as it was at Corinth.

According to the divine order, all ministries and gifts are to be exercised through love. Unless the gifts of the Spirit operate through love, a vital dimension of the Christian faith is left out. That was what happened among the Corinthian Christians. Their problems were the same as ours. Men and women were prone to self-importance as they are now. There were jockeying for position, jealous over another's eminence, or anxious to impress others with their gifts and abilities. They were more interested in the place they occupied in the church than in showing a spiritual attitude and a genuine concern for others. They loved imperfectly as we do.

With a profound insight, Paul contrasted redemptive love with those aggressive realities that make up life in this world—envy, impatience, unkindness, bragging, pride, self-centeredness, self-seeking, holding of grudges, keeping a score of wrongs, and gloating over the failures and sins of others. As Christians our protection against these things, which inevitably end in aggression against others, is Christ. In Him, we are set free by grace to love. The Holy Spirit enables us to experience the deep love of God in Christ and to express His love for others. Love begets love. We love because God loves us and has given us the capacity to love. The power of love is not something reserved for the future but is available to any one of us who will submit himself to the reign of Christ.

Spiritual gifts, which are ours through the Holy Spirit, are vital to the ministry of the Church. But the "more excellent way" is the gifts plus love. Along with faith and hope, love will never end, but the gifts of the Spirit will cease when Christ comes again. Until then, both love and the gifts are needed. The spiritual gifts are a channel through which to express God's love.

Divine love is vastly superior to any human love. When our life is transformed by Christ's life in us, it becomes more than human love. As children of God, we are lifted out of our old self-centered life, and we respond to God's redeeming love by loving Him and others. At times, we fail to show consistent goodwill toward others. This is why we are never at a place where we do not need to look to Christ for help and love.

There is nothing greater in the world than the love of God being lived out in human life. How different the history of the Church and individual lives would have been if preeminence had been placed on love! Love strengthens the bonds of the Christian community; it considers the welfare of the entire body of believers when expressing itself in the congregation and is willing to receive correction; it is humble and submits itself to duly constituted authority in the congregation.

Those who exhibit God's love long for the day when all hatred, prejudice, animosity, and strife will be things of the past; the day when people will live side-by-side in harmony; the day when God's children will see their Savior face-to-face. All the children of God are called to demonstrate His love in this suffering world until that day.

CHAPTER 9

THE FINAL REDEEMED ORDER
(15:1-58)

The goal of divine order in the Church is to prepare Christians for a new redeemed order of life—an order that will encompass the Church and all of creation. The fate of creation is intimately tied to man's fate. Adam fell and the world fell with him. As a result of Adam's sin, "creation was subjected to frustration" (Rom. 8:20 *NIV*). At the end of this age, creation will be transformed into a new and redeemed order. When redemption is complete, all creation, as well as the believers, will be transformed. This is the meaning of Romans 8:21: "That the creation itself will be liberated from its bondage to decay and brought into the freedom and glory of the children of God" (*NIV*). Freeing creation from the shackles of death is clearly a reversal of the disaster caused by Adams's fall.

At His first coming, Christ became flesh and suffered and died that He might rescue fallen people. He will visit humankind again to finish His work of redemption for the whole creation. For God who "was in Christ, reconciling the world unto himself" purposed to sum up in Christ all things in heaven and earth (2 Cor. 5:19; Col. 1:20). Creation itself waits in hope for the revelation of the children of God (Rom. 8:19). Present conditions will not continue indefinitely. The time will come when God will restore a perfect order. All things will be transformed and made new. There will be a new order of humankind, delivered from sin and death. The final redeemed order will include a perfect race of people resurrected to eternal life.

Before turning to what Paul said in 1 Corinthians 15 about the future life of believers, we may briefly consider what prompted him to devote a long chapter to the nature of the Resurrection. His teaching on the resurrection of the dead had been challenged, but the exact view of his opponents is difficult to determine.

It is quite possible that the apostle fought a war on two fronts. There could have been some in the Corinthian church who embraced the popular Greek notion of the immortality of the soul rather than the resurrection of the body. The Greeks thought the body was an evil prison in which the soul was confined. Death was seen as the occasion when the soul was liberated from the shackles of the body and was absorbed into the divine form from which it had come. Immortality was an escape from the body.

Attracted to Greek wisdom as many of the Corinthians were, some did not find it easy to accept the Christian view of eternal life that involved the whole person, body and soul. Apparently some in the Corinthian church believed that after death a person would suffer the loss of self and individuality and the soul would be absorbed into deity again. Their bodies would be gotten rid of once and for all.

Paul refuted this false teaching. For him, the Resurrection assured Christians that all that makes someone a person will survive and that his body will be transformed when Christ returns in glory. The dead will not exist without a body. The whole person will be raised. He will receive a body new in kind, "a heavenly spiritual body."

At Corinth, Paul must have defended the resurrection of the dead still on another front. Certain ones held that the Resurrection had already past. They behaved as though the kingdom of God had fully arrived. Indeed, with biting irony, Paul said, "Already you have all you want! Already you have become rich! You have become kings!" (1 Cor. 4:8 *NIV, 1984*). Like Hymenaeus and Philetus, they believed the Resurrection had already taken place (2 Tim. 2:18). The basis for this was not a denial of the resurrection of Christ from the dead; but due to the presence of the Spirit and inspired experiences they hastily concluded that the new life had already come. They thought death was behind them and that only the life of glory remained. They believed there was no such thing as a future resurrection for the faithful but only a spiritual resurrection, which they had already receive through experiences in the Spirit. They denied the bodily resurrection, insisting that all the benefits of salvation were a present reality and that there was nothing more for them in the future.

Over against this view, Paul set the Christian hope that God will give the believer a body appropriate for the life of Resurrection. Death has not yet been completely conquered. That will come in the future when Christ returns. Then salvation will touch the whole person; he will be transformed and receive a new body.

Paul met the errors of the Corinthian skeptics by calling attention to the first Easter, on which the whole Gospel rests.

THE RESURRECTION OF CHRIST

To deal with the difficulties over the Resurrection in the Corinthian church, Paul began by asserting the reality and centrality of Christ's resurrection from the dead.

The Fact (1 Cor. 15:1-11). Paul directed the attention of the Corinthians to what they should never have forgotten; namely, the Gospel that he had preached to them. It was this Gospel they had received and on which they had taken their stand. Through the Gospel, they were saved and given stability. Their salvation depended entirely on the message Paul had preached. They were to hold firmly and tenaciously to it. Otherwise, they were believing in vain.

The Gospel did not originate with Paul. He received what he had delivered to the Corinthians.[1] The message he proclaimed to them was the message of the primitive church in her earliest days. The content of the message was this:

That Christ died for our sins according to the Scriptures, that He was buried, that He was raised on the third day according to the Scriptures, and that He appeared.[2]

Among the Corinthians were those who were uncomfortable with Easter. Because of this, Paul focused on two historical facts: Christ's resurrection and His appearances. The focal center of the good news was the sacrificial death and resurrection of the Son. Both were confirmed by His burial. Only a man who was really dead would have been buried and raised. Death and burial were not the final lot of Christ. He was raised on the third day, leaving empty the tomb where His body was placed. He could not be held in bondage by death. The verb form (*egēgertai*, meaning "was raised") stresses the abiding powers of His resurrection. That stupendous miracle proclaimed the saving power of His death. He died and was buried, but no longer is He dead—no longer is He in the grave. He is alive and bestows life on all who believe in Him.

---

[1] The terms Paul used for *receive* (*paralambanō*) and *deliver* (*paradidomi*) were the customary idiom for receiving and transmitting oral tradition or doctrine. The apostle had received the Gospel from others and had handed it on to the Corinthians. His message about Jesus as the Messiah came to him by direct revelation on the road to Damascus (Gal. 1:16); he had not received it from men nor through a human mediator (Gal. 1:1). But this does not preclude the probability that he learned important facts about the life, death, and resurrection of Christ from eyewitnesses of the Lord's earthly ministry. Three years after his conversion, Paul went to Jerusalem and talked with Peter and James (Gal. 1:18-19). Later he was in that city again and met with the "pillars" of the church—James, Peter, and John. They must have shared with him what they knew about the life of Christ.

[2] These were elements of a Christ creed. A number of Biblical scholars believe that Paul cited here one of the earliest Christian creeds.

Christ's triumph over death was itself a fact of history. There were a number of disciples who saw Him after He was raised from the dead. What they saw were actual and real appearances of the resurrected Christ. The apostle presented a list of the witnesses:

"He appeared to Cephas, and then to the Twelve. After that, he appeared to more than five hundred of the brothers at the same time. . . . Then he appeared to James, then to all the apostles, and last of all he appeared to me also" (vv. 5-8 NIV).

Paul did not claim that the list was exhaustive, but his purpose was to show that Christ's resurrection was attested by individuals and by groups of varying sizes. If not all, most of them belonged to the Christian community.

The Resurrection appearances reminded Paul that he, too, had seen the risen Lord. "Last of all" Christ had appeared to him while he was on his way to persecute the Christians in Damascus. There was something unnatural about it, for the Lord appeared to him "as to one abnormally born" (*NIV*).[3] This means Paul had not been a disciple during the lifetime of Jesus. His spiritual birth and call to be an apostle were not according to the normal process. The twelve apostles had been taught by Jesus and prepared for their work. Instead of having time to mature for his ministry as they had, Paul was suddenly changed by the risen Christ from a persecutor into an apostle. The appearance of the risen Christ brought him into the Christian life.

---

[3] The *King James Version* reads "as of one born out of due time." The Greek term *ektrōma* here signifies a kind of premature birth such as an abortion or miscarriage. It is likely that Paul took the word from his opponents who used it to disparage him as a Christian and apostle. Paul's use of *ektrōma* does not suggest that as a Christian and apostle he came into being early. In fact, he was converted and called to be an apostle later than the other apostles. What *ektrōma* means in 1 Corinthians 15:8 is that the apostle had not companied with Jesus during His ministry, nor was he instructed by the Lord as the other apostles had been. He had been called to his apostleship without the normal time for maturing for such work.

Like Peter and the others, he saw the risen Christ. This was not a visionary experience. He actually came face-to-face with Jesus, who already had risen from the dead and was exalted as Lord. There was no doubt about the reality of the confrontation. It completely changed the course of his life. That he had persecuted the Church was well known, but through the risen Christ he found that grace was greater than his sin. He laid no claim to being a self-made man. It was only by the grace of God that he was a Christian and an apostle. God's bestowal of grace had not been in vain. He had labored more zealously that the others who saw the resurrected Lord. Central to the ministry of Paul and the other apostles was the proclamation, "Jesus is alive!" Historic experience verified that fact.

The Importance (15:12-19). The skeptics at Corinth said there was no resurrection of the dead. Among them could have been those who believed that the soul at death was stripped of the burdensome body and received up into heaven. So salvation was for the immortal soul, but the resurrection of the body was unthinkable. Others could have held that the Resurrection had already happened. They, too, denied the resurrection of the body, insisting that it was only spiritual—a resurrection from a life of sin into a life of righteousness.

What if they were right? What would be the conclusions? The apostle did not hesitate to point out what they were. To deny Christ's resurrection was, in effect, to deny the resurrection of believers. If there was no resurrected Lord, the apostles had preached about a dead Christ, and the Corinthians had believed in a dead Savior. Their preaching and faith had been empty and vain (vv. 14, 17). A dead Christ meant, therefore, that believers were still in their sins (v. 17), that those who were dead had perished (v. 18), and that those living were to be pitied (v. 19). They could not expect to receive anything from a dead man. But if Christ was alive, then the apostolic preaching of the Resurrection should not have been called in question (v. 12). The resurrection of Christ proved that future resurrection was a possibility.

Paul reversed his line of argument. The denial of the resurrection of believers was a denial of the resurrection of Christ (vv. 13, 15-16). There is a vital link between Christ's resurrection and that of the believers. The two are inseparable. One finds its meaning in the other. Neither can be had without the other. Belief in one implies belief in the other. To deny the resurrection of Christ is to destroy the Gospel. Without His resurrection, believers have no hope of resurrection.

THE HOPE OF THE BELIEVER

The Christian hope in life after death rests on Christ's own resurrection. That Christ arose from the dead shows the resurrection of the believers is harmonious with the redemptive purpose and power of God.

The Risen Christ Was the Firstfruits (vv. 20-28). Christ was described as "the firstfruits of those who have fallen asleep" (*NIV*) in death.[4] *Firstfruits* was a harvest term. In Palestine in the first century the firstfruits were the actual beginning of the harvest.[5] They were the initial portion of the harvest and were offered to God as a token that the entire crop was dedicated to Him. They were part and guarantee of the whole that was to follow. Christ's resurrection was the firstfruits of the Resurrection harvest, the initial portion of the whole. His resurrection represents the actual beginning of the resurrection of believers. Their resurrection is the subsequent and full harvest of His resurrection. Paul viewed these two resurrections not so much as two events but as two episodes of the same event.

---

[4] The apostle Paul characteristically spoke of those who died as those who were asleep (1 Thess. 4:13, etc.). *Sleep* was a common term for death in both Greek and Hebraic literature. As Paul used it, the term had no reference to the sleep of the soul between death and resurrection.
[5] See Ex. 23:19; Lev. 23:10; Num. 15:20f; Deut. 18:4; 26:2, 10.

At the same time, he maintained a time distinction between the two. Christ was delivered from death on the third day after His crucifixion, but the followers of Christ have not yet been raised. God began to defeat death by raising Christ. Those united to Christ by faith are assured by His resurrection of their own. Thus, as all in Adam die, so all in Christ will be made alive. The events of the End-time will proceed according to the divinely appointed order. "But each in turn, Christ, the firstfruits; then, when he comes, those who belong to him. Then the end will come, when he hands over the kingdom to God the Father" (vv. 23-24 *NIV*).

There is a proper sequence of events leading up to the End. The first, the resurrection of Christ, has already occurred. But contrary to what some thought at Corinth, the resurrection of Christians is still to come. God's redeemed people will be raised at the second coming of the triumphant Lord. At that time, those who belong to Him and have died will be brought to life. There will follow the thousand-year reign of Christ (Rev. 20:5, 12-15). During His reign, one enemy after another will be subdued. He will continue to reign until all of His enemies—rulers of darkness and hostile spiritual powers—have been conquered. Ultimate and final victory will come when the last adversary, death, is robbed of its power (1 Cor. 15:26).[6] "Then the end will come, when he hands over the kingdom to God the Father" (v. 24 *NIV*).

Of course, the *End* refers to fulfillment but not to termination.[7] It does not mean the ending of a departed state but the arrival of a perfect one. This is the goal of redemption—the divine order reestablished in the whole of creation, in which sin, Satan, and

---

[6] Paul used the word *destroy* (*katageō*) to signify not so much "annihilate" as "rob of power." Death will no longer be an effective enemy of God and His redeemed people. But it is possible that God may use it as an instrument against those whom He sees fit to punish.

[7] Paul did not discuss the general resurrection (the "resurrection of judgment" in John 5:29) in the series of events mentioned in 1 Corinthians 15. For him, this fell under the general concept, the End.

148

death are abolished. It is difficult to imagine a world where the rule is not decay and death. The final act of the divine drama will bring the redeemed order of life. In this new order, God's children will be transformed, and the world will be entirely freed of corruption, decay, and death.

When all evil powers have been put under Him and all things have been made new, Christ will deliver His kingdom over to the Father. There will be no further need for Him to reign. His mission will have been fully accomplished, and He will hand back to His Father the government of the universe. All will have been finally and fully removed that separated a holy God and a sinful world. The ground for this is Christ's victory, already won in His death and resurrection. His victory over death was the firstfruits of the abolition of death and the guarantee that the time will come when there will be no more death.

Belief in the Resurrection Had Practical Implications (vv. 29-34). The apostle Paul invited his readers to consider a custom that prevailed at Corinth—baptism for the dead.[8] Whether the Corinthians had practiced that rite is not clear since he spoke in the third person. But he did show that those who baptized for the dead were inconsistent and foolish, if the dead did not rise at all. Why did they do such a thing if there was no future life and no resurrection? It is not that Paul approved the practice or saw any value in it; he merely referred to that rite which was then in vogue and which revealed inconsistency in doctrine and practice. If the dead were beyond help, there was no point in taking any action in their behalf.

Paul turned to his own experience (vv. 30-32). He had taken tremendous risks for the sake of the Gospel. He asked the

---

[8] There are numerous interpretations of Paul's reference to baptizing the dead. Perhaps it was a local custom to baptize a relative of one who died unbaptized, with faith in Christ. Perhaps this was one of the matters that Paul wanted to set in order when he returned to Corinth (1 Cor. 11:34).

question, "Why do we endanger ourselves every hour?" (*NIV*) if there is no resurrection of the dead. He lived in jeopardy constantly. Day by day he was exposed to death, often risking his life, as he had at Ephesus, for the sake of the Gospel.[9] Unless his view of life after death was true, such a life of self-denial was utterly foolish. For Paul, the Christian life was rooted and grounded in faith. If death were merely the end, he might as well have followed the pagan philosophy: "Let us eat and drink, for tomorrow we die" (*NIV*).

Denying the Resurrection and its meaning, the Corinthians were slipping into this point of view. They were becoming corrupt and sinning against God. Therefore, the apostle warned them with these words: "Do not be misled: 'Bad company corrupts good character.' Come back to your senses as you ought, and stop sinning; for there are some who are ignorant of God—I say this to your shame" (vv. 33-34 *NIV*).

The Corinthians had fallen into this attitude about conduct when they did not lay hold on the full meaning of the resurrection of Christ. They had deliberately cultivated "bad company" (10:27)—pagan friends who denied the Resurrection and lived by the philosophy "Let us eat and drink." Their denial of the Resurrection made them one with the pagans. Speaking to them, Paul said, "There are some who are ignorant of God" (v. 34). They had forfeited their spiritual insight, and the moral consequences were regrettable. The Resurrection was and remains the basis of Christian fellowship. Christ's victory over death was pledge and guarantee of the believers' resurrection to eternal life: "Because I live, you also will live" (John 14:19 *NIV*).

---

[9] It is not likely that Paul meant that at Ephesus he had fought with literal wild beasts (*thēriomachō*). The term was used in describing gladiator contests. The apostle was a Roman citizen, and no Roman citizen was compelled to fight in an arena. Likely, Paul had in mind the abuse he received at the hands of wicked men who were ferocious and savage like wild beasts. Observe that in the catalog of afflictions he made no mention of beasts (2 Cor. 11:23-29).

THE RESURRECTION OF THE BELIEVER

So far, Paul has answered those who denied the resurrection of the dead. The next stage of his exposition dealt with the *how* of the Resurrection. "How are the dead raised? With what kind of body will they come?" (1 Cor 15:35 *NIV*). Feeling that such questions were senseless, he exclaimed "How foolish!" His point was that the future life could not be described in terms of present experience; he sought to explain to those who found it hard to accept his view of life after death something of the how of the Resurrection.

The Resurrection Body and the Mortal Body (vv. 35-41). To indicate the difference between the kinds of bodies, Paul used three analogies from nature:[10]

(1) In horticulture, a seed is put in the ground and dies; but when it germinates, it comes forth a new body (vv. 34-38). There may be something similar about the seed and the plant, but they are different. The beauty and glory of the plant are much greater than the planted seed. Likewise, the resurrected body will be more glorious than the present body. The body that is raised will not be the same as the one buried. There is a close link between them: the personality traits will be the same. But one body is buried in the ground, and another will be raised. They will be different.

(2) All flesh is not alike. There is one kind of flesh for humans, another for animals, another for birds, and another for fish (v. 39). God has given to each living creature a body suitable for its particular place in creation. Man's present body is made for life

---

[10] Salvation is applicable to the whole man, not just his soul or spirit. For Paul, the body signified not only the physical structure of man, but his total personality. The apostle's line of reasoning makes it clear that bodily existence is essential to human existence. The body is vital for the expression of the human personality. That of a man's soul and body that makes him a man will survive, but he will be changed. There is an indissoluble link between the earthly, physical body and the celestial, spiritual body.

on this earth. So it follows that God will give the believer a body that is suited for the glorified state.

(3) There are earthly bodies, and there are heavenly bodies. In earth and in heaven are bodies differing in degrees of glory. The planetary bodies that appear in the firmament—as the sun, the moon, and the stars—each have a splendor peculiar to themselves. So do men who are capable of possessing both a mortal and immortal body. God has demonstrated that He has power to create both earthly and heavenly bodies that are radically different. Thus, it is reasonable to expect the present bodies of believers to differ from their glorified bodies. Not all bodies are alike.

The Natural Body and the Spiritual Body (vv. 42-44). The resurrection of the dead means transformation. The old life gives way to the new so that believers receive bodies far superior to their present bodies.

This is made clear in the series of contrasts that follows:

"The body that is sown [buried] is perishable, it is raised imperishable; it is sown in dishonor, it is raised in glory; it is sown in weakness, it is raised in power; it is sown a natural body, it is raised a spiritual body" (vv. 42-44 NIV).

The resurrected body of the believer will stand in contrast to his present body. The difference will be due to the power of God. No longer will his body be mortal, dishonored by sin and weak. The redeemed child of God will be a new being. Can anyone imagine a body without weakness? or sickness? or disease? or death? This is a body totally unknown now to earthly existence.

The resurrection of Christians will be glorious beyond comprehension. Their bodies will be fitted for eternal life. In verse 44, Paul summed the contrast of the two kinds of bodies by saying, "it is sown a natural body [*sōma psychikon*], it is raised a spiritual body [*sōma pneumatikon*]." The Greek word here for *natural* is derived from the word *psychē*, which means "life" or "soul." "A natural body" is not made of soul (*psychē*), but is animated by the soul. It is the body in its present form and with which man is clothed during his life in this age. Too, "a spiritual body" is not made of spirit (*pneuma*), but is the new body, animated by the Spirit of God. The spiritual body will be completely transformed and empowered by the Holy Spirit. It will be the perfect instrument of the Spirit and adapted for existence in the redeemed order of the age to come. The spiritual body is as much a part of the divine economy as is the natural body. Each performs its function in the divine order.

The First Adam and the Last Adam (vv. 45-49). To continue his discussion of the two kinds of body, the apostle chose the heads of two different families: the first Adam and the last Adam. All people belong to the family of Adam, but the family of the second Adam, Jesus Christ, consists of all believers. Adam is described literally as "a living soul" (*psychē*); that is, his existence was altogether on the level of natural human life. As a result, Adam and all of his children have had natural bodies. But the last Adam is called a "life-giving spirit" (*NIV*), which points to the spiritual body. Christ in His resurrection entered into a new order of existence. His body was animated by the Spirit of God, and He took into the presence of God His resurrected, glorified body.

Developing his argument further, Paul set forth God's final redeeming act in Christ that made it possible for people to receive spiritual bodies. The first man was a natural, earthly man created out of the dust. He transmitted to his children the earthly. Generation after generation each has inherited a "natural" dying body. In contrast, the second Man was not from the earth but from heaven. However, He came in the form of an earthly man, bearing a "natural" mortal body, and He suffered and died for the sins of the world. At His second coming, Christ will visit humankind again to transmit the heavenly to believers and to finish His work of redemption for all creation. Just as all people bear in their bodies the image of the earthly, so shall those who have been adopted in God's family bear His spiritual image forever.

As the risen Christ had a glorified body, so also will Christians. Speaking of the return of Christ, Paul said the Lord "will transform our lowly bodies so that they will be like his glorious body" (Phil. 3:21 *NIV*). In this age "we share in his suffering in order that we may also share in his glory" (Rom. 8:17 *NIV*). The expectation of the Christian was summed up well by the words, "Christ in you, the hope of glory" (Col. 1:27). Believers one day will share in Christ's glory; even their bodies will be similar to His glorious body.

THE DISCLOSURE OF A MYSTERY

A divine mystery had been disclosed to Paul about what was to happen at the End. So he drew his exposition of the Resurrection to a close by noting that what had happened to Christians by faith was not the final resurrection. This event will happen when the Lord comes for the Church.

The Change of the Believer's Body (1 Cor. 15:5-54). The body of the believer must be transformed from its present condition to be suited to the eternal kingdom of God. "Flesh and blood cannot inherit the kingdom of God, nor does the perishable inherit the imperishable" (v. 50 *NIV*). "Flesh and blood" refers to living people, and is not applied to the dead. The reference is made to the natural man as a frail, mortal creature.[11] The term *perishable* is used for corpses in decomposition.

The contrast of verse 50 is one between those who will be alive at the second advent of Christ and those who will have died before His return. Neither will be able to take part in the

---

[11] Compare Matthew 16:17; Galatians 1:16; Ephesians 6:2; Hebrews 2:14.

kingdom of God as they are. The living and the dead must both experience transformation and be provided with a new spiritual body—a resurrection body of glory.

A change is necessary. When the Lord Jesus comes for the Church, there will be a sudden and glorious change.

We will not all sleep, but we will all be changed—in a flash, in the twinkling of an eye, at the last trumpet. For the trumpet will sound, the dead will be raised imperishable, and we will be changed. For the perishable must clothe itself with the imperishable, and the mortal with immortality (vv. 51-53 NIV).

This is the blessed hope for all Christians. Those who have fallen asleep will, at the return of Christ, be raised in glorified bodies; and those who are living will experience the transformation of their bodies into a glorified state. The living and dead "in Christ" will experience the same change.

The Conquest of Death (vv. 55-57). Confident of ultimate victory over death, Paul mocked death as though it was already conquered:

Where, O death, is your victory? Where, O death, is your sting? (v. 55 NIV).

Death is more than a physical occurrence, for it has a sting because of sin. It is punishment and an evil that need not exist. It was man's rebellion against his Creator that introduced death into his experience.

Moreover, a close link exists between sin and the Law. The apostle Paul said the power of sin is the law of God (v. 56). The Law makes us aware of what is right and wrong; it defines sin and condemns it. Though it is holy, righteous, and good (Rom. 7:12), the Law offers us no power to do good and avoid evil. It declares to us the claims of God.

Paul was certain of victory over sin and death. Because Christ satisfied the demands of the Law, it has no power to condemn those who are clothed in His righteousness. There is no condemnation to those who are in Christ Jesus (Rom. 8:1). When He comes again, those who have died in Him will be rescued from death and ushered into the glorious life of the Resurrection. The resurrection of Christ is a pledge and the beginning of victory over death, but victory will not be fully won until the End (1 Cor. 15:26). Anticipating it, the apostle exclaimed, "But thanks be to God! He gives us the victory through our Lord Jesus Christ" (v. 57 *NIV*).

The Resurrection is the foundation of the Christian hope. Let us therefore be steadfast and immovable in our conviction regarding the Resurrection. Let us abound in the work of the Lord, being fully assured that our labor will not be in vain, but will ultimately win the victory with Him who overcomes all things.

CONCLUSION

Christianity is an Easter faith. Without Easter morning, the world probably would never have heard of Jesus Christ. His victory over death made the early Christians aware that the power of death is not the only possible conqueror. There is One stronger, and He has prevailed as the conqueror of death.

The grim reality and sorrowful experience of death cannot be glossed over. When confronted by death, unsaved people often find themselves destitute of hope. But the Church has a clear message for the utter hopelessness of the world. Only the message that Christ has risen can give hope to the ones who face certain death. He and He alone died and arose again from the grave. His triumph over death is the foundation of the believer's hope of resurrection after death. The resurrection of Christ and the resurrection of believers belong together, the first being the "firstfruits" and the guarantee of the second.

The tomb did not mark the close of Christ's life. Nor does it mark the end of those who belong to Him. At His coming, both the believers who are still alive and those who have died will "be caught up . . . to meet the Lord in the air" (1 Thess. 4:17). Their bodily, earthly existence will be transformed by God's glory. They will be new people. The weaknesses and deformities that sin has laid on them will be destroyed. No longer will they be subject to death; they will be recast and transformed for redeemed existence on this earth.

God will restore a perfect order, with a perfect race of men and women, bearing the divine image. The redeemed will live in a world entirely free of sin, decay, and death (Rom. 8:19-21). This means nothing less than a complete transformation of all human existence. Christ's redemptive work will reach beyond believers and encompass the entire creation. When Christ has subjected the whole world to Himself, He will deliver this redeemed order to God the Father. The children of God will understand this fully when they enter into the life of glory, but it is hard to imagine a world without sin, suffering, and death. Yet what is now almost unimaginable lies in the future for the believer!

What no eye has seen, what no ear has heard, and what no human mind has conceived—the things God has prepared for those who love him—these are the things God has revealed to us by his Spirit (1 Cor. 2:9-10 NIV).

SELECTED BIBLIOGRAPHY

Arrington, French L. *New Testament Exegesis: Examples.* Washington, D.C.: University Press of America, 1977.

_____. *Paul's Aeon Theology in 1 Corinthians.* Washington, D.C.: University Press of America, 1977.

Barclay, William. *The Letters to the Corinthians.* Philadelphia: Westminster Press, 1956.

Barrett, C. K. *The First Epistle to the Corinthians.* Harper's New Testament Commentaries. New York: Harper and Row, 1968.

Bauer, Walter, William F. Arndt, and F. Wilber Gingrich. *A Greek English Lexicon of the New Testament and Other Early Christian Literature.* Chicago: University of Chicago Press, 1961.

Blass, Frederick, and Albert Debrunner. *A Greek Grammar of the New Testament and Other Early Christian Literature.* Translated and revised by Robert W. Funk. Chicago: The University of Chicago Press, 1961.

Bornkamm, Günther. *Paul.* Translated by D. M. G. Stalker. New York: Harper and Row, 1971.

Conn, Charles W. *A Balanced Church.* Cleveland, Tennessee: Pathway Press, 1975.

Conzelmann, Hans. *A Commentary on the First Epistle to the Corinthians.* Hermeneia. Translated by James W. Leitch. Philadelphia: Fortress Press, 1975.

Cross, James A. *A Study of the Holy Ghost.* Cleveland, Tennessee: Pathway Press, 1973.

Cullmann, Oscar. *The Early Church.* Translated by A. J. B. Higgins and Stanley Godman. Philadelphia: The Westminster Press, 1966.

Gale, Herbert M. *The Use of Analogy in the Letters of Paul.* Philadelphia: The Westminster Press, 1964.

Gray, James Comper, and George M. Adams. *Gray and Adams Bible Commentary.* Grand Rapids: Zondervan, n.d.

Héring, Jean. *The First Epistle of St. Paul to the Corinthians.* Translated by A. W. Heathcote and P. J. Allcock. London: The Epworth Press, 1962.

Horton, Stanley M. *What the Bible Says About the Holy Spirit.* Springfield, Missouri: Gospel Publishing House, 1976.

Hughes, Ray H. *What Is Pentecost?* Cleveland, Tennessee: Pathway Press, 1963.

Hurd, J. C. *The Origin of 1 Corinthians.* New York: Seabury Press, 1965.

Kwiran, Manfred. *The Resurrection of the Dead.* Basel: Fredrick Reinhardt Kommissionserlag, 1972.

McPheeters, Julian C. *The Epistles to the Corinthians.* Grand Rapids: Baker Book House, 1964.

Moffatt, James. *Commentary on 1 Corinthians.* London: Hodder and Stoughton, 1938.

Munck, Johannes. *Paul and the Salvation of Mankind.* Translated by Frank Clark. Richmond: John Knox Press, 1959.

Robertson, Archibald, and Alfred Plummer. *A Critical and Exegetical Commentary of the First Epistle of St. Paul to the Corinthians.* International Critical Commentary. Edited by S. R. Driver and others. Edinburgh: T. & T. Clark, 1914.

Roetzel Calvin J. *Judgment in the Community.* Leiden: E. J. Brill, 1972.

Spittler, Russell P. *The Corinthian Correspondence.* Springfield, Missouri: Gospel Publishing House, 1976.

Triplett, Bennie. *A Contemporary Study of the Holy Spirit.* Cleveland, Tennessee: Pathway Press, 1970.

Wagner, C. Peter. *A Turned-On Church in an Uptight World.* Grand Rapids: Zondervan Publishing House, 1971.

Whitley, D. E. H. *The Theology of St. Paul.* Philadelphia: Fortress Press, 1972.